PARIS

FLYING HIGH

WHITE STAR PUBLISHERS

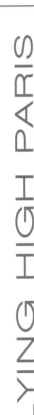

FLYING HIGH PARIS

PHOTOGRAPHS

Philippe Guignard

Text
DOMINIQUE PAULVÉ

Project Editor
VALERIA MANFERTO DE FABIANIS

Graphic Design
PAOLA PIACCO

Cover
The Cathedral of Notre-Dame.

Back cover
Île de la Cité.

1
The Tour Eiffel reaches towards the sky.

2-3
The Île Saint-Louis and the Île de la Cité.

4-5
The shiny new modernity of the Beaugrenelle quarter.

Contents

6-7
The Arc de Triomphe.

8
The dome of Les Invalides.

9
Place du Tertre, in Montmartre.

10
The Pont Neuf spans the Seine, crossing the Île Saint Louis.

11
The Grande Arche de la Défense.

12-13
The pipes on the exterior of the Centre Pompidou are colored according to their function: blue for air, green for fluids, yellow for electricity, and red for flow and safety.

14-15
The Carreau des Halles.

16-17
The third platform of the Tour Eiffel.

PHILIPPE GUIGNARD WAS BORN IN BRITTANY IN 1957. HE HAS EXTENSIVELY TRAVELED THE CONTINENTS PRODUCING PHOTOGRAPHIC AND VIDEO DOCUMENTARIES FOR INTERNATIONAL COMPANIES. DURING HIS TRAVELS HE HAS BUILT UP A TREASURY OF IMAGES BASED ON METROPOLITAN DEVELOPMENT, URBAN LANDSCAPES AND ARCHITECTURE. FOR ABOUT TEN YEARS, HE HAS SPECIALIZED IN AERIAL IMAGES OF FRANCE AND IN 2001, HE LAUNCHED THE AIR-IMAGES AGENCY, WHICH SPECIALIZES IN AERIAL PHOTOGRAPHY. CURRENTLY, HIS VIEW OF ARCHITECTURE AND URBAN DEVELOPMENT FOCUSES ON INSTITUTIONAL COMMUNICATION, EDITING AND THE PRESS. THIS BOOK IS HIS SECOND ONE FEATURING PICTURES TAKEN OVER PARIS.

20-21
The Hôtel de Ville (City Hall) is one of Paris' most majestic buildings.

22-23
The Ministry of Foreign Affairs and the Palais Bourbon,
which houses the National Assembly.

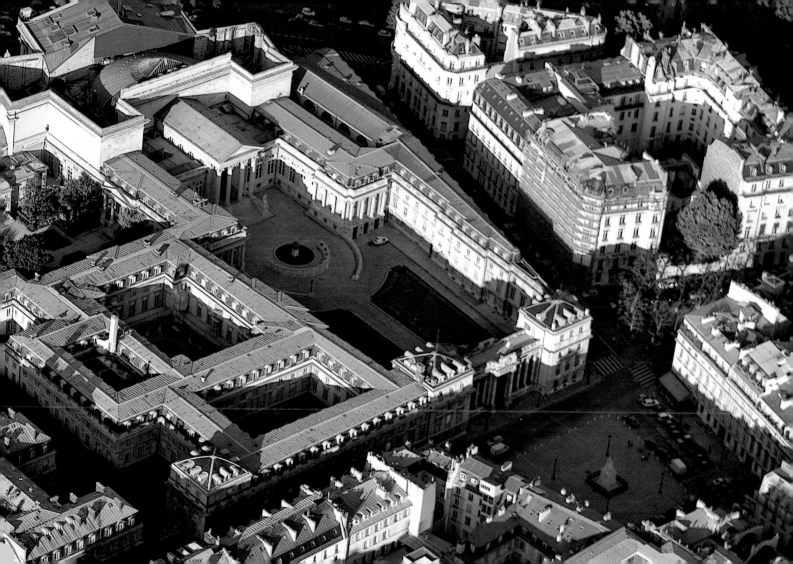

FLYING HIGH PARIS

Introduction

———

PARIS IS A FASCINATING CITY THAT, UNLIKE MANY OTHER GREAT METROPOLIS-
ES, BEGAN AS A COLLECTION OF VILLAGES, WHICH ARE STILL DISCERNABLE TO-
DAY. AT STREET LEVEL EACH *ARRONDISSEMENT* CONVEYS ITS OWN DISTINCTIVE
ATMOSPHERE, WITH ITS ACTIVITIES GROUPED ACCORDING TO TYPE WITH DIS-
TRICTS CONTAINING OFFICES, DEPARTMENT STORES, ART GALLERIES, "TOURIST"
QUARTERS WITH FAMOUS MONUMENTS, SURROUNDED BY LIVELY RESTAURANTS
AND BOUTIQUES, AND SO ON. THE CITY ALSO OFFERS THE ALLURE OF HUGE
PARKS, NUMEROUS SQUARES CONTAINING PUBLIC GARDENS, AND HISTORIC
CEMETERIES, WHERE GREAT ARTISTS HAVE SCULPTED IMMORTAL WORKS OF
STONE OR BRONZE IN MEMORY OF OTHER ARTISTS OR ILLUSTRIOUS DIGNITARIES.
THEN THERE IS THE LAYOUT OF PARIS ITSELF, WHICH WAS FOUNDED ON THE ÎLE
SAINT-LOUIS AND THE ÎLE DE LA CITÉ, AND SUBSEQUENTLY DEVELOPED ALONG

24
The Sacré-Cœur Basilica dominates the capital
from the top of Butte Montmartre.

Introduction

THE BANKS OF THE SEINE, GRADUALLY SPREADING OUT ON TWO OPPOSITE SIDES, THE RIVE DROITE AND THE RIVE GAUCHE.

WHO COULD HAVE IMAGINED THAT WHAT WOULD LATER BECOME THE VILLE LUMIÈRE COULD HAVE ORIGINATED ON AN UNREMARKABLE LITTLE ISLAND IN THE MIDDLE OF THE SEINE? DURING THE 3RD CENTURY BC THERE WAS NOTHING BUT A CLUSTER OF HUTS MADE FROM BRUSHWOOD AND REEDS INHABITING WHAT IS NOW KNOWN AS THE ÎLE DE LA CITÉ. THE ISLAND WAS INHABITED BY A COLONY OF PRIMITIVE PEOPLE WHO HAD SETTLED ON THIS MARSHY SCRAP OF LAND. IT WAS, NONETHELESS, PERMANENTLY ABOVE WATER AND THEY SURVIVED BY FISHING IN THE RIVER AND THE OXBOWS HIDDEN IN THE FORESTS ON ITS SHORES. THIS TRIBE, KNOWN AS THE *PARISII*, WAS ONLY A VERY MINOR POPULATION OF ANCIENT GAUL, BUT THEY SKILLFULLY USED THE CONDITIONS OF THE ISLAND TO THEIR ADVANTAGE. THE ÎLE DE LA CITÉ OCCUPIED A STRATEGIC POSITION THAT RENDERED IT A FIXED CROSSING POINT FOR THE BOATMEN USING THE RIVER THAT SEPARATED THE TWO HALVES OF GAUL. THE TIMBER, SUPPLIED BY THE SUR-

Introduction

ROUNDING WOODED HILLS (WHICH LATER BECAME KNOWN AS MONTMARTRE, MONTAGNE SAINTE-GENEVIÈVE AND BELLEVILLE), WAS USED TO BUILD TWO WOODEN BRIDGES THAT JOINED THE ORIGINAL NUCLEUS OF PARIS TO THE BANKS OF THE SEINE. THE *PARISII* WERE ASTUTE MERCHANTS AND TOOK ADVANTAGE OF THE BRIDGES TO IMPOSE TAXES ON THE GOODS CROSSING THEM. THE SEINE IS THE BACKBONE OF PARIS, WHICH IT CROSSES, ENLIVENS AND IRRIGATES. INDEED, THE CITY'S COAT OF ARMS DEPICTS A BOAT ON THE WATER SURMOUNTED BY FLEURS-DE-LIS AND ACCOMPANIED BY THE MOTTO *FLUCTUAT NEC MERGITUR,* "TOSSED BY THE WAVES, SHE DOES NOT SINK." PARIS WAS THUS FOUNDED ON A SCRAP OF LAND, BUT THE EXPANSION OF THE CITY AND ITS SUBURBS HAS CONTINUED CEASELESSLY SINCE CLOVIS I, KING OF THE FRANKS AND SUBSEQUENTLY OF FRANCE, GRANTED ITS NOBLE TITLES.

PARIS CAN BE VIEWED IN DIFFERENT WAYS. THE VISITOR CAN CHOOSE TO ADMIRE AN AERIAL VIEW OF PART OF THE 41 SQUARE MILES (66 SQUARE KILOMETERS) OF THE CITY FROM THE 3RD STORY OF THE TOUR EIFFEL, 905 FEET (275 METERS)

FLYING HIGH PARIS

28
The magnificent, recently restored glass structure
of the Grand Palais.

ABOVE THE GROUND. VIEWING PARIS FROM THE TOP OF THE CITY'S BUILDINGS AND MONUMENTS, AS YOU CAN DO FROM THE MASSIVE ARC DE TRIOMPHE, AL-LOWS AN APPRECIATION OF THE HARMONIOUS LAYOUT OF THE CHAMPS-ÉLYSÉES. IT LEADS TO THE PLACE DE LA CONCORDE ON ONE SIDE, AND THE AVENUE DE LA GRANDE ARMÉE, WHICH RUNS FOR ALMOST A MILE AND A HALF TO THE GRANDE ARCHE DE LA DÉFENSE, ON THE OTHER. THE PANORAMIC VIEW OF PARIS FROM THE 56TH FLOOR OF THE TOUR MONTPARNASSE IS UNRIVALLED, ALTHOUGH NOT FOR THOSE WHO SUFFER FROM VERTIGO! THE TERRACE OF THE SACRÉ-CŒUR BASILICA IN MONTMARTRE IS ANOTHER PRIVILEGED SPOT OFFERING A WONDER-FUL VISTA OF THE CITY EXTENDING IN ALL DIRECTIONS.

HOWEVER, ADMIRING PARIS FROM THE SKY IS A DIFFERENT ADVENTURE ALTO-GETHER, ONE IN WHICH THE PEDESTRIAN CANNOT PARTICIPATE. ALONE IN HIS HELICOPTER ABOUT 1000 FT (305 M) ABOVE THE BUSTLING METROPOLIS, PHILIPPE GUIGNARD ENJOYS A UNIQUE VIEW: OTHERWISE INVISIBLE TERRACES, GLEAMING ROOFTOPS AND ALL KINDS OF ARCHITECTURAL DETAILS HIDDEN FROM THE EYES

Introduction

OF THE PARISIAN PEDESTRIAN. INDEED, APART FROM BIRDS, WHO ELSE CAN CLAIM TO BE FAMILIAR WITH THE GLISTENING MODERNITY OF THE APEX OF I.M. PEI'S PYRAMID, THE HIDDEN GARDENS OF LE MARAIS, THE MASONRY OF THE OPÉRA, OR THE FINE DETAILS OF THE GÉNIE DE LA BASTILLE? GUIGNARD, AND NO ONE ELSE, CAN SEE ALL OF THIS AND MUCH MORE BESIDES. VIEWED FROM ABOVE, PARIS SEEMS A SMALL CITY (DESPITE ITS AREA OF 41 SQUARE MILES, COMPRISING THE BOIS DE VINCENNES AND THE BOIS DE BOULOGNE, WHICH ARE OFFICIALLY CONSIDERED PART OF THE CAPITAL) WITH AN AMAZING AMOUNT OF GREEN AREAS. THE BIRD'S-EYE VIEWS ALSO REVEALS SOME OF THE STRATIFICATION OF THE CITY, WHICH GREW UP OVER THE COURSE OF MANY CENTURIES. HOWEVER, AERIAL PHOTOGRAPHY OF PARIS IS POSSIBLE ONLY AT CERTAIN TIMES OF DAY AND IN CERTAIN SEASONS, BECAUSE OF THE LIGHT. FURTHERMORE, GUIGNARD IS ALSO CONSTRAINED BY THE LIMITED NUMBER OF FLIGHT HOURS THAT HE HAS BEEN ABLE TO OBTAIN AUTHORIZATION FOR, IN ORDER TO FLY OVER THE CITY. PARIS WAS NOT BUILT IN A DAY, AND THE SAME IS TRUE FOR THIS BOOK,

Introduction

WHICH HAS REQUIRED SEVERAL YEARS OF PAINSTAKING WORK AND DOZENS OF FLIGHTS. HOWEVER, THE RESULT IS THAT WE ARE ABLE TO SEE THE MOMENT WHEN NOTRE-DAME'S MULTICOLORED ROSE WINDOWS ARE IMMORTALIZED AT THEIR MOST DAZZLING. WE CAN SEE WHEN A STRANGE SHADOW GIVES THE BUREN COLUMNS A MYSTERIOUS ATMOSPHERE, OR WHEN THE IRIDESCENT HUES OF THE WATERS OF THE SEINE, VIEWED IN THE MORNING, FULLY DESERVE BAUDELAIRE'S FAMOUS VERSE,

L'AURORE GRELOTTANTE EN ROBE ROSE ET VERTE

S'AVANÇAIT LENTEMENT SUR LA SEINE DÉSERTE

ET LE SOMBRE PARIS, EN SE FROTTANT LES YEUX

EMPOIGNAIT SES OUTILS, VIEILLARDS LABORIEUX...

"SHIVERING DAWN IN A ROBE OF PINK AND GREEN

MADE HER WAY SLOWLY ALONG THE DESERTED SEINE,

AND SOMBER PARIS, EYES RUBBED AND WATERING,

GROPED FOR ITS TOOLS, AN OLD MAN, LABORING."

32
The 144-foot Colonne Vendôme rises in the center of Place
Vendôme, the masterpiece commissioned by Louis XIV.

THEN THERE ARE THE INNER COURTYARDS OF PRIVATE BUILDINGS THAT ARE STUDDED WITH FLOWER-BORDERED POOLS, THE ENTHUSIASM OF VISITORS TO THE TOUR EIFFEL, CRAMMED BEHIND THE PROTECTIVE GRILLES AND THE (RARE) SOLITUDE OF A PEDESTRIAN BENEATH THE ARC DE TRIOMPHE: THESE ARE THE BEAUTIFUL GLIMPSES FROM ABOVE THAT WE WISH TO SHARE WITH YOU. BACK ON THE GROUND, THEY WILL UNDOUBTEDLY INSPIRE YOU TO VIEW THE CITY'S LAND-MARKS DIFFERENTLY. PERHAPS YOU WILL CROSS NEW THRESHOLDS, OR VENTURE A LITTLE FARTHER AFIELD, ALMOST TO THE OUTSKIRTS, WHERE THE GREAT CON-TEMPORARY ARCHITECTS HAVE LEFT THE IMPRINT OF THEIR TALENT AND MODER-NITY ON A CITY FAMOUS FOR THE BEAUTY OF ITS CENTURIES-OLD BUILDINGS.

34-35
Saint Germain des Prés is Paris' renowned writers' quarter.

36-37
Les Invalides is a peaceful haven in the center of Paris.

38-39
Only the dazzling white Sacré-Cœur Basilica emerges from the
shadow cast over the cityscape by the mass of clouds.

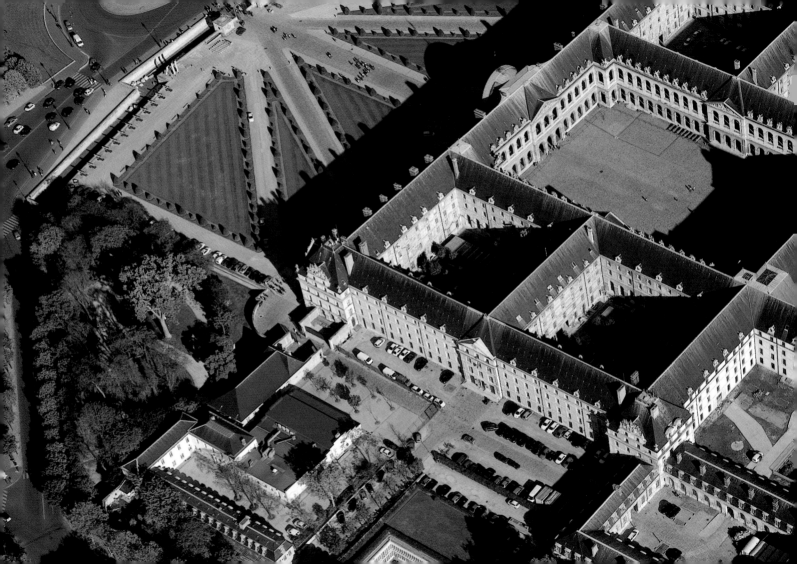

THE ISLANDS AND LE MARAIS:
THE INFANCY OF PARIS

FLYING HIGH

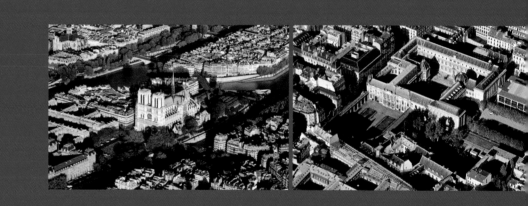

FLYING HIGH PARIS

41

Notre-Dame Cathedral rises majestically in the center of the Île de la Cité (left). Le Marais is a quarter noted for its fine and well-proportioned mansions.

A walk around the Île de la Cité and the Île Saint-Louis, in the heart of Paris, is undoubtedly the most romantic stroll offered by the French capital. The Seine islands are bounded by the Pont Neuf, surmounted by a statue of Henri IV in armor, on one side and Pont Sully, on the other. The starting point for exploring them is the legendary Place Dauphine, lined with brick and stone houses and shaded by ancient horse-chestnut trees. The Palais de Justice (Law Courts) complex stands next to the square, on a ten-acre site, comprising the Conciergerie and the Sainte-Chapelle. This Gothic chapel is an architectural masterpiece with 15 superb stained-glass windows and a huge rose window depicting the Apocalypse.

Notre-Dame is one of the world's largest cathedrals and one of the most visited monuments in Paris. It overlooks a huge square and attracts over 12 million tourists every year. Visitors can ascend the 402 steps that lead to the top of the towers to enjoy unrivaled views of the city and to admire the stone tracery, carved gargoyles and other fantastic figures adorning the façade. Behind the cathedral, tourists can rest on the benches in Place Jean XXIII, among impeccably manicured box hedges. Pont Saint-Louis is the smallest of Paris' bridges and connects the Île de la Cité with the Île Saint-Louis. Rue Saint-Louis en l'Île is the main street of the island of the same name, which it divides almost exactly in half. This is one of those Parisian "villages" in which there is no room for modernity. Taking a stroll here is like stepping back in time, due to the magnificent 17th-century mansions, balconies, ancient signs and artistic wrought-iron decorations.

42

The Île Saint-Louis is connected to the Île de la Cité by the Pont Saint-Louis pedestrian bridge.

The Islands and Le Marais:
the Infancy of Paris

It is only a short distance as the crow flies to the quarter of Le Marais, with its grandiose Place des Vosges, built at the beginning of the 17th century by Henri IV. It is not known who conceived this well-proportioned square, but its beauty lies in the unified design: the houses are the same height and impeccably aligned, with blue slate roofs, white limestone and red brick façades, and identical small-paned windows. Only two pavilions rise above the unified roofline: the Pavilion of the King, and the Pavilion of the Queen, which face each other on opposite sides of the garden. Arcades run around the buildings and house antique shops and various stores and restaurants. In the center of the square are the gardens known as Square Louis XIII, where the local children gather. This little park is adorned with trees, lawns, fountains and an equestrian statue of Louis XIII cast by Jean-Pierre Cortot and Louis-Marie Dupaty in 1825. The quarter surrounding Place des Vosges is dotted with many splendid mansions, now divided into apartments or owned by various authorities.

The Centre National d'Art et de Culture Georges Pompidou, inaugurated in 1977, stands on the Rue Beaubourg, which marks the edge of Le Marais. It is named after the French president, who founded it with the intention of creating a museum dedicated to contemporary-art culture in Paris. After winning an international competition, architects Richard Rogers and Renzo Piano were commissioned to design the building. Their goal was to construct a revolutionarily modern structure in one of the oldest quarters of the capital. With huge floors, whose internal layout can be altered according to display requirements; a metal and glass exterior; ducts and pipes in contrasting

The Islands and Le Marais:
the Infancy of Paris

colors; and an escalator resembling a huge red snake, the Centre Pompidou aroused great controversy before being "adopted" by hundreds of thousands of visitors. On the opposite side of Boulevard Sébastopol, a modern complex has been built on the site of Les Halles, once the city's central market: the Forum des Halles, designed by architects Claude Vasconi and Georges Pencréac'h in 1979.

Place du Jour is the site of the church of Saint-Eustache, a handsome Gothic building renowned for its fine organs. Closer to the Hôtel de Ville (City Hall), whose Renaissance-style façade was faithfully reconstructed after having been burned by the Commune in 1871, is the Neoclassical building of the old Halle aux Blés (Grain Exchange). It was built at the end of the 18th century and was subsequently converted into the Bourse de Commerce (Commercial Exchange). A little further towards the Seine lies the Place du Châtelet, which leads to the Pont-au-Change. The Théâtre du Châtelet and the Théâtre de la Ville, both built in the Italianate style by Gabriel Davioud in 1862, face each other across the square, while the "Palm Fountain," commissioned by Napoleon from François-Jean Bralle in 1806, adorns its center.

One of the most handsome squares in Paris is undoubtedly Place Vendôme, ordered by Louis XIV and built during the same period as the Place des Victoires. In the center stands the 144-ft (44 m) Vendôme Column topped with a statue of Napoleon. The square is lined with magnificent buildings that are home to the Ministry of Justice, the famous Hôtel Ritz (the Parisian residence of the Sultan of Brunei) and world-famous jewelry stores. Place des Victoires (formerly known as

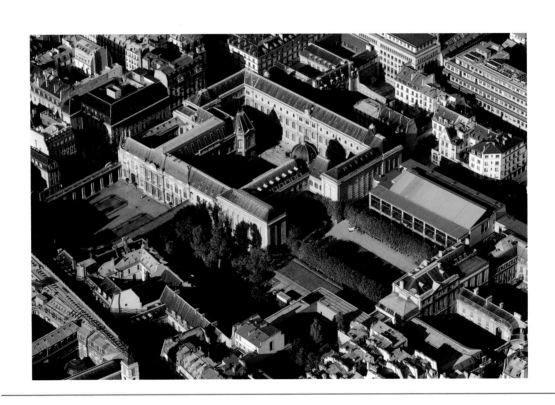

FLYING HIGH PARIS

46

The National Archives, housed in the former Hôtel de Soubise, have gradually spread to the neighboring buildings and now occupy an area of 323,000 square feet (30,000 sq m) in the Marais quarter.

Place Louis XIV), like Place Vendôme, was designed by Jules Hardouin-Mansart. Although the buildings lining the square – originally private houses, built between 1685 and 1883 – have lost part of their harmony due to the opening of new streets, they still retain a certain charm and are now home to the boutiques of top designers.

The gardens of the Palais Royal are exceptionally beautiful. This 5-acre rectangle of greenery is ideal for a pleasant stroll, commencing at the Buren columns. Amid lawns and avenues of red horse-chestnut trees, the American landscape designer Mark Rudkin has created flowerbeds in the style of an English country garden that are a feast for the eyes during springtime. However, visitors to Paris often choose to commence their tour of the city in its most famous museum, on the right-bank of the Seine: the Ensemble du Palais du Grand Louvre, which rises between the glass pyramid erected by I.M. Pei in 1988 and the marble and bronze Arc de Triomphe du Carrousel, commissioned by Napoleon I.

The arch frames glimpses of the Tuileries Gardens and the view up the Champs Elysées toward the Arc de Triomphe. It is a delight to succumb to the allure of Paris with a stroll through the Carrousel Gardens, admiring the statues by Maillol, followed by the tranquility of the Tuileries. Here you can walk among pools and flowerbeds, where sculptures by Rodin, Laurens and Germaine Richier flank works by Penone, Lichtenstein and Louise Bourgeois.

FLYING HIGH PARIS

48
The Île de la Cité and the Île Saint-Louis are reached via the Pont Neuf and Place
Dauphine and resemble a huge boat anchored in the Seine.

50 and 51
Of Paris' 37 bridges across the Seine, 12 connect the Île Saint-Louis and the Île de la Cité, which would otherwise be isolated from the rest of the city.

52
The Fountain of the Virgin is visible among the greenery of Place Jean XXIII, behind Notre-Dame.

53
Pont Sully, connecting the Rive Droite and the Rive Gauche, touches the tip of the Île Saint-Louis.

FLYING HIGH PARIS

55
Notre-Dame, one of the world's greatest cathedrals, stands on the edge of the Île de la Cité.

56 and 57
It is a pleasure for the eye to linger on Notre-Dame's symphony of stone, which is mesmerizing at any time of day.

58 and 59
Whether viewed from the front or the side, the sunlight illuminates the countless architectural details of the cathedral, emphasizing its rose windows and fine stone tracery.

60-61

Only an aerial photographer can admire the purity of Notre-Dame's windows and flying buttresses.

62 and 63
The view of Paris from the top of Notre-Dame's towers – reached by climbing 402 steps – is unique, and the pedestrians in the square below resemble ants.

FLYING HIGH PARIS

65
The 213-foot spire (65 m) of Sainte-Chapelle towers over the Palais de Justice.

66 and 67
An aerial view reveals the triangular shape of the Place Dauphine, which is overlooked by the Palais de Justice and its monumental steps. The gardens of the pretty little Square du Vert-Galant, shaded by trees, can be seen on the right.

68 and 69
No modern buildings mar the well-proportioned architecture of the Île Saint-
Louis, where even the tallest mansions
merge with the landscape.

70-71
Viewed from the Rive Gauche, the
Place Dauphine and the Palais de
Justice form an imposing complex.

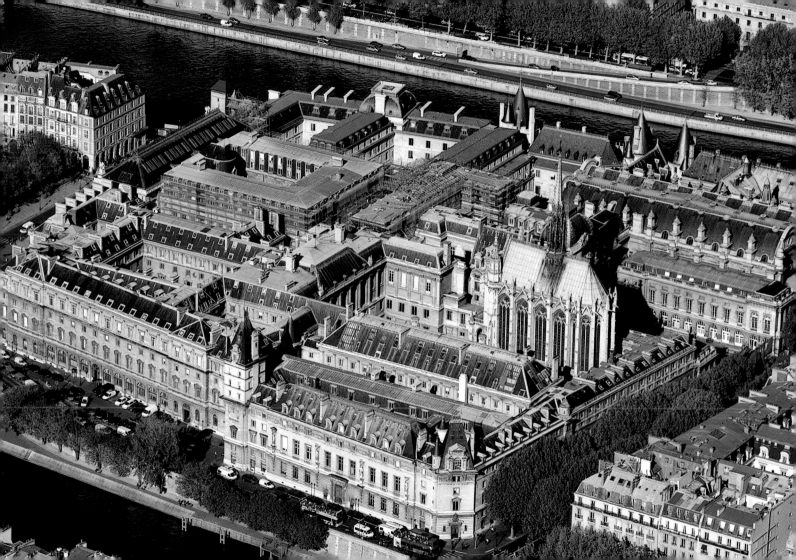

FLYING HIGH PARIS

73
Commissioned by the Prince de Soubise at the end of the 18th century, the building
that bears his name was designed by the architect Pierre-Alexis Delamair.

FLYING HIGH PARIS

74
The regal Place des Vosges, commissioned by Henri IV, was inaugurated in 1612. The Pavilion of the King and the Pavilion of the Queen face each other across the square, rising above the surrounding buildings.

76 and 77

The majesty of Place des Vosges is partly due to the impeccable alignment of its 34 identical buildings, which emphasize the Pavilion of the
Queen (opposite the Pavilion of the King). In the center is the garden with
one of the four fountains designed by Jean-Pierre Cortot.

78 and 79
As in the rest of Le Marais, some of the mansions on the Rue du Parc Royal have been painted brick red to imitate the façades of the nearby Place des Vosges.

80

The Tribunal Administratif de Paris is housed in the Hôtel d'Aumont, whose façade overlooking the garden was redesigned by François Mansart in 1656.

81

The exterior of the church of Notre-Dame des Blancs-Manteaux (belonging to the Servite Friars) was designed by Victor Baltard in 1863.

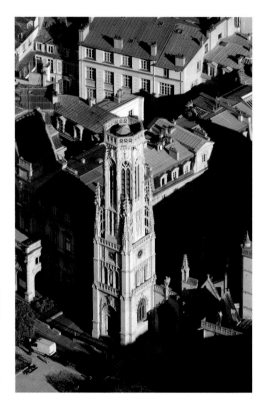

82
The church of Saint-Germain l'Auxerrois is one of the oldest in Paris and boasts a handsome Romanesque tower dating from the 12th century.

83
The architecture of Saint-Gervais-et-Saint-Protais is unusual among Parisian churches, as it superimposes the three classical orders: Doric, Ionic and Corinthian.

FLYING HIGH PARIS

84

The Conservatoire National des Arts et Métiers (National Conservatory of Arts and Crafts) is the oldest institute of higher education in France after the Sorbonne and was founded in 1794. It forms a huge complex in the 3rd *arrondissement* of Paris, and comprises great halls, libraries, study rooms, a museum and even a chapel.

86 and 87
In 1867 the H-shaped city hall of the 3rd arrondissement was built in the République quarter on the site originally occupied by the Temple prison and subsequently by the first "ultramodern" Parisian laundry, commissioned by Napoleon III.

88
Separated by inner courtyards, the buildings of the National Library of France, in Rue Vivienne, stand opposite the pretty Louvois garden, whose box hedges, acacia trees and ancient horse chestnuts form an island of greenery in the quarter.

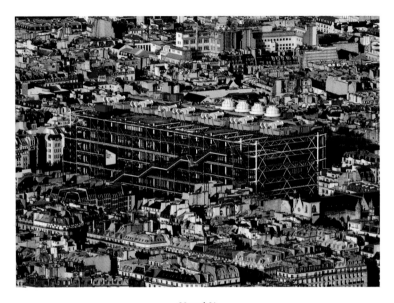

90 and 91
Inaugurated in 1977, the Centre National d'Art et de Culture Georges Pompidou was conceived as a giant construction kit by the young architects Richard Rogers and Renzo Piano, together with Gianfranco Franchini.

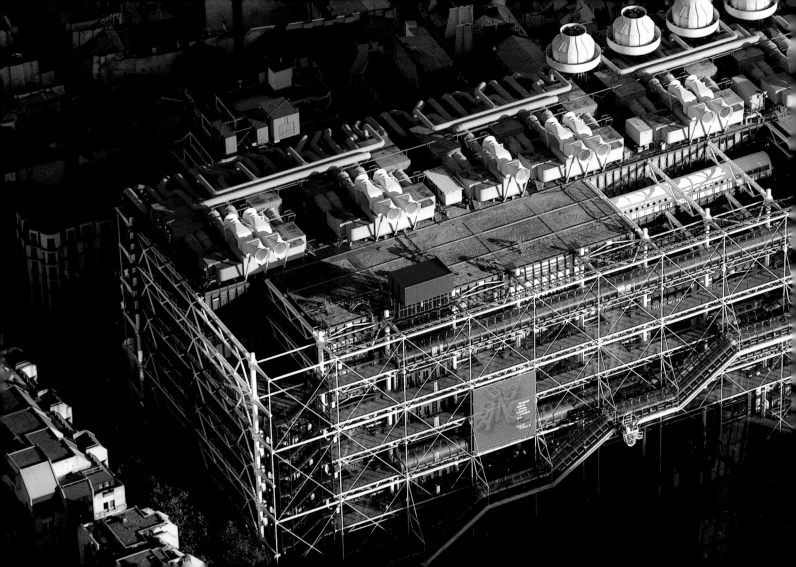

92-93

Known locally as Beaubourg, the building is 150 feet tall (45 m) and has an area of over 1,108,000 square feet (103,000 sq m). It is served by escalators, whose zigzagging course is visible from the outside.

FLYING HIGH PARIS

95
The huge metal structure of the Centre Pompidou, with multicolored pipes and ducts
housing its essential inner workings, attracts the eye in this aerial view.

96-97
The Forum des Halles is Paris'
largest shopping center. It was designed by Claude Vasconi and
Georges Pencréac'h in 1979.

98
The edges of the huge "crater" of the Forum des Halles are surrounded by glass with white-painted metal arches.

99
The roofs of the pavilions resemble up-turned umbrellas and were designed as light wells.

100
At 345 feet long (105 m), 140 feet wide (43 m) and 112 feet tall (34 m), Saint-Eustache is Paris' largest church after Notre-Dame.

101
The dome of Paris' Bourse de Commerce has been listed as a historical monument since 1986.

FLYING HIGH PARIS

102
Place René Cassin, conceived as a contemporary maze by architect Louis Arretche, is located in the center of the Jardin des Halles. *Ecoute*, a Burgundy sandstone sculpture by Henri Miller, can be seen in the foreground.

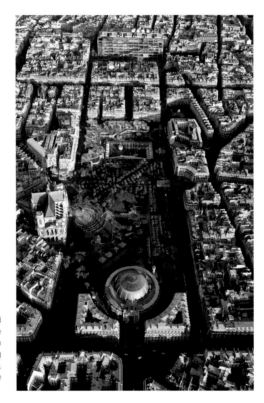

104 and 105
South of the Jardin des Halles, the old Grain Exchange has been home to the Bourse de Commerce since the mid-18th century. This unusual circular building boasts fine windows and a metal dome, which gleams in the sunlight. The dome was built in 1813 and restored in 1889.

107
This view of Paris, with the Pont-Neuf in the foreground, extends from the Louvre to the Gare de Lyon.

108
Many different plant species are grown in the airy Square du Vert-Galant, which forms a pretty green triangle on the tip of the Île de la Cité.

109
Viewed from above, the two pavilions over-looking the entrance to Place Dauphine emphasize the square's fine architecture.

110 and 111
The fortunate inhabitants of the Île Saint-Louis need only step outside their doors to enjoy a stroll along the Seine to watch the *Bateaux Mouches* gliding along the river.

112 and 113

Sous les ponts de Paris coule la Seine... and also the Bateaux Parisiens that can be boarded at Port de la Bourdonnais, at the foot of the Tour Eiffel. In the photograph the boats can be seen passing beneath the Pont Sully and along the Quai des Orfèvres.

114-115

The façade of the Hôtel de Ville, rebuilt in the Renaissance style in 1882, is adorned with 378 works sculpted by artists including Rodin and Boucher.

116-117
The flower market, held in Place Louis Lépine is a green island between the Prefecture of Police and the Hôtel-Dieu. The dome of the Tribunal de Commerce rises in the center of the photograph.

118-119
The façade of the Palais de Justice overlooking Place Dauphine is adorned with a series of white stone columns and was inspired by the Dendera Temple in Egypt.

120 and 121
The Théâtre de la Ville (formerly known as the Théâtre Sarah Bernhardt) and the Théâtre du Châtelet in place du Châtelet were built by Gabriel Davioud, one of Baron Haussmann's collaborators. In the center, the fountain by François-Jean Bralle is surmounted by a gilded bronze Victory.

122-123
This view shows the rooftops of the church of Saint-Germain l'Auxerrois, the houses lining the Quai de la Mégisserie, and the La Samaritaine department store.

124 and 125
La Samaritaine is named after the first hydraulic pump installed in Paris
near the Pont Neuf, which was decorated with a relief of the Good
Samaritan. Its façades, built in the Art Nouveau style by Frantz Jourdain
between 1903 and 1907, were enriched with Art Deco motifs during
restoration by Henri Sauvage in 1933.

126 and 127
The Vendôme Column is formed by a spiraling series of 425 bronze plates depicting trophies and ancient battles and is topped with a statue of Napoleon by August Dumont. It stands in the center of one of Paris' finest squares.

128-129
The beautiful proportions of Place Vendôme can be fully appreciated from above. The handsome buildings lining the square were designed by renowned architects, including Jacques V Gabriel and his son Ange-Jacques Gabriel, Jules Hardouin-Mansart and Germain Boffrand.

FLYING HIGH PARIS

131
When important guests are expected in Place Vendôme, the traditional red carpets are rolled out to greet them.

132
The apartments of the Palais Royal, whose arcades have long housed old-fashioned boutiques and elegant modern stores, enjoy views over this carefully arranged garden.

134
On warm summer days people cool off around the pools in the garden.

135
In 1986 Daniel Buren installed his famous columns in the forecourt of the
Palais Royal, attracting much criticism. Pol Bury's metal sphere fountains
can be seen behind the colonnade.

136
The circular Place des Victoires, was designed as a showcase for the equestrian statue of Louis XIV.

137
The zinc dome of the Polish church of Notre-Dame-de-l'Assomption rises above the surrounding buildings on the Rue Saint-Honoré.

138-139
This photograph shows the Musée d'Orsay (right) and the Louvre and the Tuileries Gardens (left) on the banks of the Seine.

140
The perfect alignment of the buildings of the Louvre and its Pyramid are a fitting prelude to the flowerbeds of the Carrousel and Tuileries Gardens.

141
Viewed from above, the Obelisk in Place de la Concorde resembles a pin stuck in the square.

142
Only from a helicopter is it possible to see that the large flowerbed that separates the Louvre from the Carrousel Gardens encloses the base of an inverted pyramid, situated opposite that of I.M. Pei.

143
The base of the inverted pyramid forms a "rotunda" that separates the Louvre from the Carrousel Gardens.

144
At sunset the visitors crowding around the Pyramid that forms the entrance to the Louvre look like ants.

145
The play of light and shadows on the glass panes of the Pyramid affords glimpses of the buildings around the Cour Napoléon.

146
Opposite the Arc de Triomphe du Carrousel, the inverted pyramid looks like part of a temporary installation.

147
At the time of its construction the Pyramid aroused much controversy, due to the strong contrast that it created with the historical buildings of the Louvre.

148 and 149

André Le Nôtre laid out geometric flowerbeds to enhance the views in the Tuileries Gardens. Here, in front of the octagonal pool opposite the symmetrical horseshoe-shaped Fer à Cheval, stone balustrades lead to the terraces.

150 and 151
The round pool is admirably framed by white stone Medici vases and statues by Louis-Ernest Barrias, Denis Foyatier and Paul Jean-Baptiste Gasq, which form a permanent guard of honor on the green lawns.

152

For decades the garden has been dotted with old-fashioned iron chairs, offering visitors a chance to rest around the pool.

153

Like the triumphal arches of the Roman empire, the Arc de Triomphe du Carrousel is surmounted by a bronze quadriga, flanked by a pair of Victories.

THE RIVE GAUCHE:
GREAT DOMES AND PARKS

FLYING HIGH

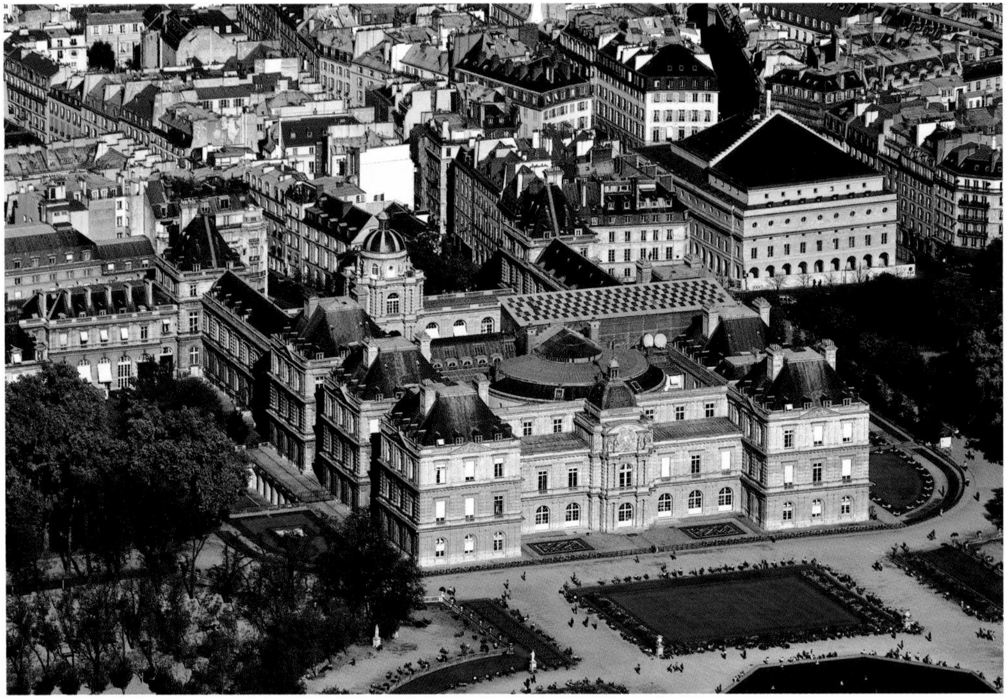

155
The Tour Eiffel (left) rises proudly on the Rive Gauche, overlooking the Seine and the Champ de Mars.
The Panthéon stands on top of Montagne Sainte-Geneviève (right).

Along with the Seine islands and Le Marais (once a marsh), the Latin Quarter is one of the capital's oldest and liveliest districts and has been the stronghold of the Parisian intellectual world since the Middle Ages. It is also the site of important churches and government headquarters. Its main street is the Boulevard Saint-Michel, which is home to the church of Saint-Séverin, hidden among the medieval atmosphere of the narrow streets. It was rebuilt in the Flamboyant Gothic style in the 13th century and is dominated by a slender bell tower that reaches toward the sky. On the opposite side of the "Boul' Mich," as the street has long been called by students, lie the well-preserved ruins of the Gallic-Roman baths of Cluny. The gateway of the Hôtel des Abbés de Cluny, next to the Roman ruins, affords a glimpse of the inner courtyard of this fine example of medieval architecture. Further along the boulevard is the Sorbonne, the emblem of French higher-education and the country's oldest university, whose buildings have been extensively rebuilt over the centuries. Behind the university stands the Lycée Louis-le-Grand, founded by Jesuits in the mid-16th century and rebuilt in 1898 by the architect Charles Le Cœur, who preserved the original façades of the main inner court. The nearby Lycée Henri-IV is famous for its tall Clovis bell tower.

Other interesting monuments and buildings are scattered over the area between the Latin Quarter and Saint-Germain-des-Prés, which is home to the Luxembourg Gardens. The park surrounds the palace of the same name, which houses the French Senate and was built by Salomon de Brosse for Marie de' Medici, and is adorned with many stone statues, pools, an api-

156
The majestic Palais du Luxembourg dominates Marie de' Medici's cherished gardens.

The Rive Gauche:
Great Domes and Parks

ary and an orangery. On the Rue de Vaugiraud it adjoins the Odéon Théâtre de l'Europe, built between 1779 and 1782 by Peyre and De Wailly to house the Comédie Française. Three important churches are located in close proximity. The first of these is the Panthéon, built on the top of the Montagne Sainte-Geneviève between 1757 and 1790. Its colossal, austere façade was modeled on the Pantheon in Rome. The inscription on the pediment reads, Aux *Grands Hommes La Patrie Reconnaissante* ("To great men, the grateful homeland"). At 62-ft (19 m) tall and 213-ft (65 m) long, with a Latin-cross plan, the church of Saint-Germain-des-Prés, towers over its famous, eponymous quarter, whose inhabitants – known as *Germanopratins* – enjoy strolling along the streets lined with antique shops, smart boutiques, cafés and restaurants.   The church of Saint-Sulpice, which has been rebuilt several times following its foundation in the 12th century, boasts a fine bell tower that is one of the tallest in Paris and a square containing a fountain, built in 1847 by Louis Visconti. The Val-de-Grâce military hospital, built in 1655, also contains a handsome church designed by François Mansart. Beyond, the beautiful Baroque architecture of the Institut de France, built by Cardinal Mazarino, stretches along the Seine, flanked by two pavilions and topped by the famous dome beneath which the French Academy meets. In order to satisfy the requests of scholars and learned men, Louis XIV and his minister of finance Jean-Baptiste Colbert decided to build the Paris Observatory on a vacant plot of high land at Port-Royal. The observatory is the oldest functioning in the world and was built by architect Claude Perrault between 1668 and 1672. In 1845 its central tower was topped with a dome, known as the Arago Dome, after the astronomer,

The Rive Gauche:
Great Domes and Parks

mathematician and physicist François Arago, who was one of the observatory's directors. Nearby is La Santé Prison, the only jail in central Paris. It was set on a trapezoidal plot by Vaudremer in 1867. The area around the Avenue de Breteuil is representative of the quiet and elegant 7th *arrondissement,* which is home to handsome apartment blocks and private palaces with hidden gardens. The wide avenues and large squares are lined with trees, creating a peaceful, luxurious atmosphere, exemplified by the Hôtel Matignon, which contains Paris' largest private garden, and the Musée Rodin. This museum is set in 7.5-acre grounds adorned with important works by the famous sculptor, such as the *La Porte de l'Enfer* ("The Gates of Hell") and *Le Penseur* ("The Thinker"). On the other side of the Boulevard des Invalides, among the courtyards and gardens, the huge Les Invalides complex houses Napoleon's

tomb, the Musée de l'Armée, a retirement home for war veterans and a military hospital. The École Militaire, at the end of the Champ de Mars, is a military school that was built during the reign of Louis XV at the suggestion of Maurice de Saxe, Marshal of France. Although it was designed by Ange Gabriel in 1751, the building was not completed until 1780 due to lack of funds.

The Tour Eiffel is one of the most-visited monuments in the world and each year 6.5 million people ascend its platforms by means of the panoramic lifts. The metal tower was erected in 1889 and was originally intended to be a temporary structure. At the top of the tower visitors can view a reconstruction of the offices of Gustave Eiffel and his engineers.

The latest large-scale architectural project to have been completed in Paris is the Musée du Quai Branly, designed by Jean Nouvel and inau-

FLYING HIGH PARIS

160
The towers of the National Library of France (the François Mitterrand site) rise
opposite the contemporary architecture of the Ministry of Finance and the Palais
Omnisports de Paris-Bercy.

gurated in June 2006. Dedicated to the art of Africa, Oceania, the Americas and Asia, the museum is set in a luxuriant garden of 200,000 sq. ft (61 sq. m) that was planned by landscape gardener Gilles Clément and planted with thousands of different species. The quarter of Montparnasse is dominated by the Tour Montparnasse, built in 1972 by Sabot, Beaudoin, Cassan and De Marine, and is home to the Cartier Foundation for Contemporary Art (1994), again designed by Nouvel.

Jean Nouvel also designed the Arab World Institute (1988), whose light-flooded glass and steel architecture is a blend of modernity and tradition. The southern façade of the building is imbued with the ancestral atmosphere of 240 *meshrebeeyehs* (balconies enclosed with lat-ticework) reinterpreted by the architect. A little further along the Seine is the oldest garden in Paris, the Jardin des Plantes, whose botanical garden, eye-catching flowerbeds, maze, greenhouses, aviaries and galleries of the Muséum National d'Histoire Naturelle occupy a site of 69 acres. It lies opposite the Gare d'Austerlitz, one of Paris' six major railway stations. The riverbank beyond is home to many restored buildings, heralding a new lifestyle and stretching as far as the modern National Library (the Bibliothèque Nationale de France, commissioned by François Mitterrand). This marks the boundary with the neighboring suburbs. These are currently the scene of fervid restoration work, with abandoned factories and warehouses rapidly being transformed into artists' studios and homes.

162
Framed by the fine buildings lining the Rue Saint-Jacques, the church of Saint-Séverin stands in the heart of the Latin Quarter.

163
Its gleaming slate roofs set off the impeccable craftsmanship of its flying buttresses.

164 and 165
Dating from the end of the 2nd century, the Gallic-Roman baths stand
next to the wall of the Hôtel de Cluny, which houses the Musée National
du Moyen-Age.

166 and 167

Built to the design of Louis Le Vau between 1662 and 1688 on the axis of the Cour Carrée of the Louvre, the semicircular façade of the building housing the Institut de France extends along the Seine like the wings of

168 and 169
The Sorbonne was rebuilt at the end of the 19th century by Henri-Paul Nénot, who preserved the chapel inaugurated in 1653. The perimeter of the area occupied by the buildings is marked by Rue des Ecoles, Rue Saint-Jacques, Rue Cujas and Rue de la Sorbonne.

170
Rue Soufflot crosses the Latin Quarter, from the Panthéon to the Luxembourg Gardens, with the Sorbonne on the left.

171
The dome of the chapel of Sainte-Ursule, built by Jacques Lemercier in 1642, was the first of its kind to be covered with slate held in place by lead ribs and punctuated with skylights.

172 and 173
Opposite the church of Saint-Etienne du Mont, the Lycée Henri-IV has remained unchanged since the end of the 18th century. The school is dominated by the Clovis bell tower and its four wings are arranged like the arms of a cross around a Baroque rotunda, forming an imposing complex.

174

The dome of the Lycée Henri-IV rises above the buildings arranged around the Cours des Externes and was restored by Jean-Baptiste Rondelet in 1790.

175

The courtyard of honor at the Lycée Louis-le-Grand, which is not visible to passersby, has an elaborate pavement.

176 and 177
The Ministry of Higher Education and Research is housed in a complex linked by gardens in Rue Descartes. A statue by the surrealist artist Meret Oppenheim stands in the center of the Cour Carré and its large rectangular pool.

178-179
Viewed from above, the roofs of the Sorbonne are contained within the area marked by Rue de l'Ecole de Médecine and Boulevard Saint-Michel.

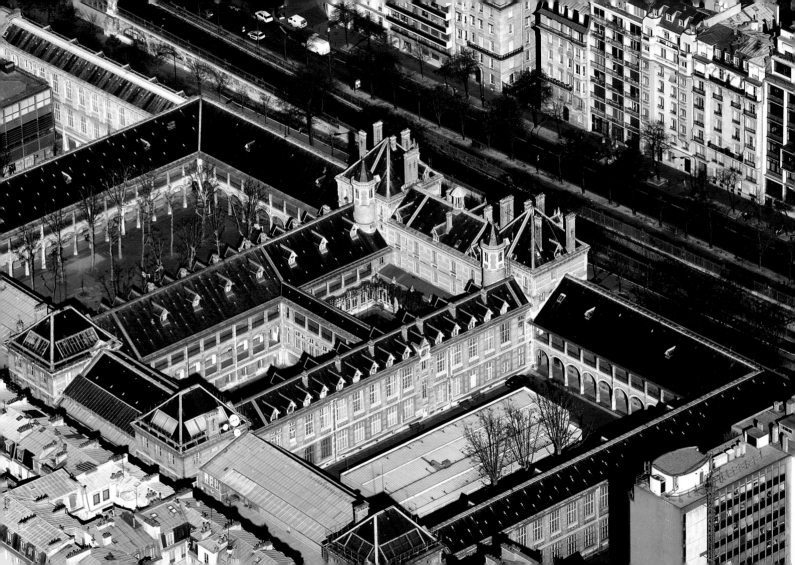

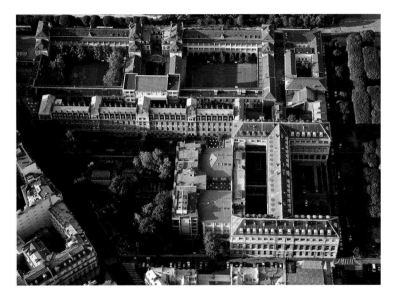

180
The Lycée Buffon, on Boulevard Pasteur, was built by Vaudemer in 1885.
The building overlooking the little court of honor is topped by eight towers.

181
Viewed from above, the Lycée Montaigne's red-tiled roofs distinguish it
from the Sorbonne and the Rectorat.

182-183
The Panthéon is the masterpiece of the architect Jacques-Germain Soufflot and dominates the city from the top of Montagne Sainte-Geneviève.

184 and 185
Consecrated to the glory of great men and the emblem of this part of Paris, the Panthéon is the soul of the Latin Quarter. Its Greek-cross plan and portico imitate an ancient temple.

186

The 22 Corinthian columns of its portico support the pediment carved with a bas-relief by David d'Angers.

187

Its famous dome, like the lantern that crowns it, was completed by Jean Rondelet in 1790, after Soufflot's death.

188 and 189
The Val-de-Grâce military hospital, which occupies the 22-acre site of the former convent of the same name, is constituted by a group of 17th-century buildings and a modern H-shaped edifice built in 1979. The dome of its Eglise Royale was designed by Gabriel le Duc and modeled on that of Saint Peter's in Rome.

190 and 191
The arcades of the Val-de-Grâce convent buildings are separated by tall columns and were designed by François Mansart. The windows of the VIP rooms open onto a garden containing flowerbeds bordered with carefully manicured box hedges. These are closed to the public.

192-193
The superb roof of the Val-de-Grâce, covered with thousands of slate tiles, appears in all its glory in this aerial photograph.

FLYING HIGH PARIS

195
The vista from Rue Soufflot towards the Seine islands reveals the handsome lines of the Boulevard Saint-Michel and the Rue Saint-Jacques.

196
The quarter is dominated by the square bell tower of Saint-Germain-des-Prés, the oldest church in France.

197
The nearby church of Saint-Sulpice was founded during the 12th century and was dependent on the church of Saint-Germain-des-Prés, which was then an abbey.

198 and 199
The Odéon theatre, renamed the Théâtre de l'Europe in 1990, was the first Parisian theatre on the Rive Gauche, and opened in 1782. Its architecture, inspired by the style of ancient temples, is characterized by restrained cubic forms.

FLYING HIGH PARIS

200
This spectacular view encompasses much of Paris, from Avenue de Breteuil to the Bois de Boulogne, showing the green areas of the 7th *arrondissement*.

202

Two square towers flank the façade of the church of Saint-François-Xavier. The building was inaugurated in 1874 and is a fine example of the architecture of its period.

203

The huge Place de Breteuil, near Les Invalides, was laid out in 1782. In its center stands an imposing monument to Louis Pasteur by Alexandre Falguière (1900).

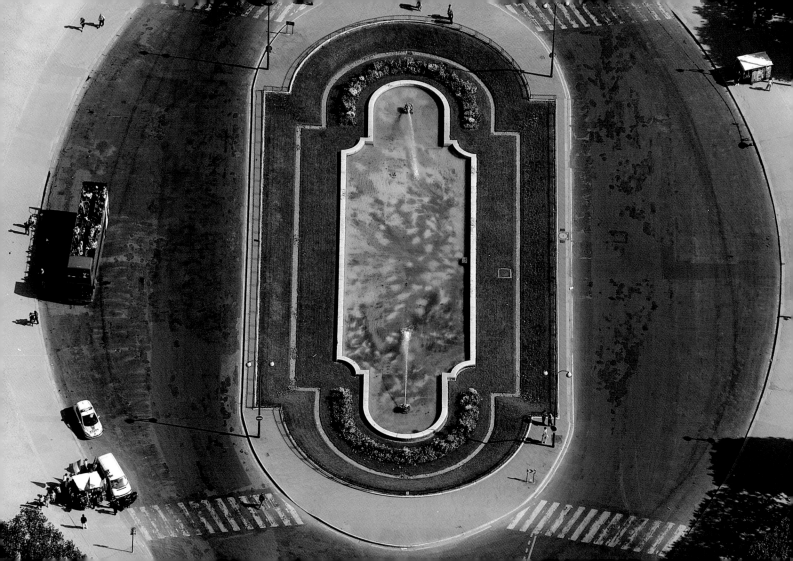

204
Place Jacques-Rueff contains a pool framed by a flowerbed and lawn and is situated in the middle of the Champ de Mars, which stretches from the Tour Eiffel to Les Invalides.

205
Le Bon Marché was founded by Aristide Boucicaut (1854) and was the world's first department store. The building that houses it was designed by Gustave Eiffel.

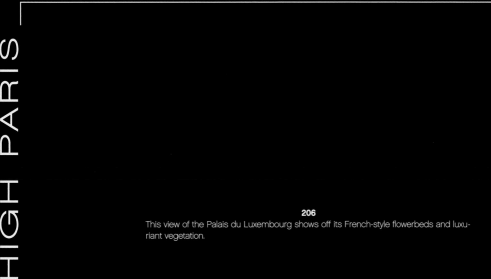

206
This view of the Palais du Luxembourg shows off its French-style flowerbeds and luxuriant vegetation.

FLYING HIGH PARIS

209
Only an aerial view can encompass the many different areas of the Luxembourg Gardens: the orchard, the orangery, the tennis courts, the children's playgrounds, the nursery, and so on.

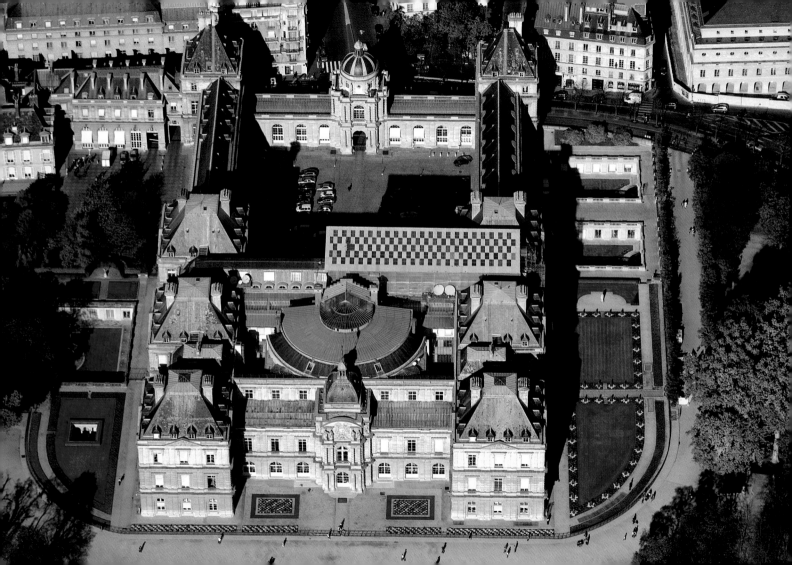

210 and 211
Built by the architect Salomon de Brosse between 1615 and 1622, the Palais
du Luxembourg was commissioned by Marie de' Medici and was modeled on Palazzo Pitti and the Boboli Gardens, where she spent her child-
hood. As in Florence, the roof of the palace has no skylights. Flowerbeds
and lawns frame the octagonal pool on the main axis of the gardens.

212 and 213
Marble statues stand in the center of circular lawns bordered with flowers. They depict figures from Greek mythology and also busts of the queens of France and famous men.

214 and 215
The 689-foot-tall (210 meters) Tour Montparnasse has 59 floors and dominates the quarter and the Gare Montparnasse, from which it is separated by Place Raoul-Dautry.

216 and 217
The terrace of the Tour Montparnasse offers breathtaking views over Paris and on clear days it is possible to see for 25 miles (40 kilometers). Orientation panels are located around the terrace, offering visitors information on the various quarters of the city and the monuments that can be seen from the tower.

218

The completely glass and metal structure of the Cartier Foundation for Contemporary Art was built by Jean Nouvel in 1994.

219

Designed by landscape gardeners François Brun and Michel Péna in 1994, the Jardin Atlantique is a green area built above the railway lines of the Gare Montparnasse.

220
The Hôtel Méridien-Montparnasse forms a circle with the Neoclassical building designed by Ricardo Bofill (1985) in Place de Catalogne and another by Maurice Novarina (1988). A fountain by Shamaï Haber stands in the center.

221
Montparnasse cemetery covers an area of 47 acres, making it one of the largest green areas in Paris.

222
Seen from the sky at dusk, the zinc roofs of this part of the 14th *arrondissement* have a powdery appearance.

223

Rue de Vaugirard is the longest street in the capital. Its rooftops extend for 14,100 feet (4,300 m), as far as the eye can see.

224
The vista corresponding to the Paris Meridian – extending from the Observatory to the Palais du Luxembourg – is visible only from the sky.

225
Louis XIV built the Royal Observatory to house astronomical instruments in 1667 at the request of the astronomer Adrien Auzout.

226 and 227
The Denfert-Rochereau quarter is home to many hospitals and nursing homes. The Hôpital Saint-Vincent-de-Paul stands on a site formerly occupied by the Oratorians. Several buildings were added around its handsome garden during different periods, the latest in 1969.

228 and 229
The Tour Eiffel is the world's most famous monument, far surpassing Versailles and the Leaning Tower of Pisa. Standing 1063 feet (324 m), it was built by Gustave Eiffel in 1889 and has dominated the city ever since.

230
This view, with the Tour Eiffel in the foreground, encompasses the dome of Les Invalides, Notre-Dame, the Panthéon and the Tour Montparnasse.

231 left
The height of the Tour Eiffel was increased by 78 feet (24 m) in 1957 with the addition of a television antenna.

231 right
The tip of the famous tower seems to cut the Trocadéro gardens into two perfect halves in this photograph.

232
The Tour Eiffel, which rises imposingly above the huge Champ de Mars, is rivaled only by the Tour Montparnasse.

233
The Tour Eiffel looms against the blue background, its first and second platforms crowded with tourists. The buildings of La Défense district can be seen in the background.

234-235
Each year over 6.5 million people ascend the famous tower, on foot or in the elevators.

FLYING HIGH PARIS

237
Around December 21st – the shortest day of the year – the Tour Eiffel appears to emerge out of thin air, in a dream-like fashion.

238 and 239

The Musée du Quai Branly was designed by Jean Nouvel, who placed brightly colored "boxes" in front of the galleries. The building is set in a garden covering an area of almost 200,000 square feet (18,000 sq m) designed by Gilles Clément and planted with thousands of different plants.

240

Like many mansions of the 7th *arrondissement*, the one that now houses the Conseil Supérieur de la Magistrature (Disciplinary Court of the Judiciary) overlooks a peaceful garden.

241

Visitors can board the Bateaux Parisiens at the Port de la Bourdonnais to cruise along the Seine, enjoying views of Paris from a new angle.

242 and 243

Construction of the church of Saint-Louis des Invalides was commenced by Jules Hardouin-Mansart in 1677. It consists of two distinct parts, the domed Royal Church and the Soldiers' Church, and forms a ruler-straight line, dominating Avenue de Breteuil as far as the square of the same name.

244 and 245
The gilded dome of the church of Saint-Louis des Invalides gleams on the Paris skyline. It rises above the Cour Royal, which is surrounded by 17 inner court-yards adorned with green gardens and flowerbeds.

246 and 247
North of Les Invalides, the courtyard opens onto a grassy esplanade
reaching towards the Seine. Sumptuously decorated antique cannons
recalling the victories of the French army flank the entrance gates.

248 and 249

The UNESCO Headquarters were built by the architects Breuer, Nervi and Zehrfuss and inaugurated in 1958. The design of the four buildings was revolutionary at the time, and the structures fit perfectly into the landscaped grounds designed by Roberto Burle Marx.

250 and 251
One of Paris' finest and most interesting museums is the Musée Rodin, housed in the Hôtel Biron, where the artist resided from 1908. Built during the 18th century and set in 7.5-acre grounds, the handsome building boasts beautifully manicured gardens adorned with works of art by the great sculptor.

252 and 253

Facing the Louvre, on the opposite bank of the Seine, the Musée d'Orsay is housed in the old railway station built by Victor Laloux in 1898. The building covers an area of 618,850 square feet (57,400 sq. m) and is topped with a zinc and glass roof.

254
Situated between the Gare des Invalides and the National Assembly, the Ministry of Foreign Affairs is housed in a building on the Quai d'Orsay designed by J. Lacornée in the sumptuous style typical of the period of Napoleon III.

256
Pont Alexandre III symbolizes the Franco-Russian alliance and was built
by architect Jean Résal for the Universal Exposition of 1900.

257
The National Assembly is housed in the Palais Bourbon, built for the
Duchess of Bourbon in 1722 by architects Giardini and Lassurance.

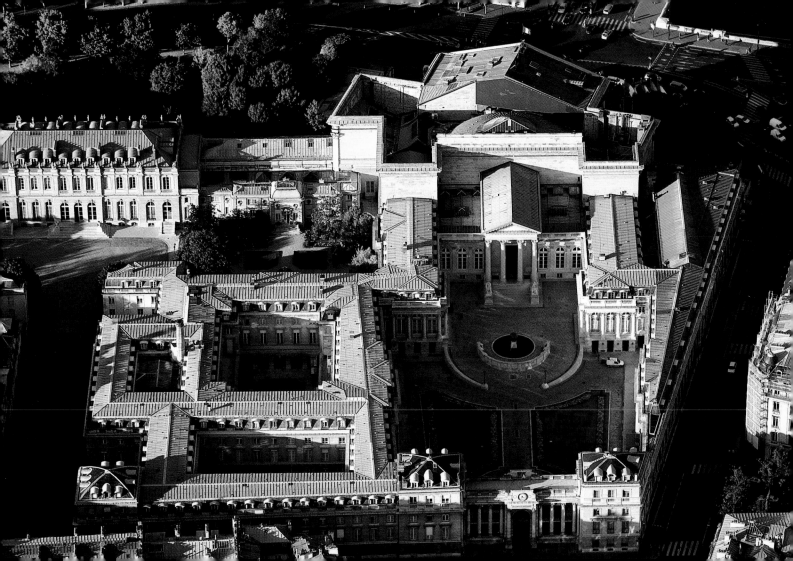

258
The State Secretariat for Overseas Affairs is situated in Rue Oudinot, in the old Hôtel de Montmorin, built at the beginning of the 19th century. The façades overlooking the inner courtyard have been re-modeled, notably by Brogniart.

259
The Jardin Catherine Labouré in the Sèvres-Babylone quarter was laid out in 1978 on the old garden of the Daughters of Charity.

260 and 261
Gardens in Rue de Babylone: that of the Society of Foreign missions is
flanked by the huge landscape garden of the Italian Embassy, while the
garden of the Daughters of Charity can be seen beyond.

262
The old Laennec Hospital was built by Christophe Guimard in 1632. It closed in 2000 and is currently being restored.

263
The Foundation of the Brothers Hospitallers of St. John of God in Rue Oudinot boasts a fine garden planted with handsome trees.

264 and 265

Hôtel Matignon, the official residence of the French prime minister since 1959, was built in 1722 by Jean Courtonne for the Prince of Tingry. A semicircular courtyard allows access to two buildings, while the 7.5 acre grounds, designed by Achille Duchêne in 1902, form the largest private garden in Paris.

266 and 267

The Jardin des Plantes is the oldest botanical garden in Paris and covers an area of 69 acres. The Carrés de la Perspective is a series of planted plots covering an area of 5 acres and extending from Place Valhubert to the Grand Gallery of Evolution of the Muséum National d'Histoire Naturelle. Formerly a zoological gallery, built in 1872, the building was restored by Paul Chemetov, Borja Huidobro and the stage designer René Allio, and reopened in 1994.

268
The vista of square gardens, in full bloom from April to the end of autumn, is edged by a double avenue of plane trees.

269 left
Visitors can admire ancient trees and rare plants along the winding paths of the Labyrinth.

269 right
Built in brick and stone by Molinos in 1812 to house large animals, the Rotonde is surrounded by five pavilions.

270

With its *ryiad* (patio), pools, fountains
and 108-foot (33 m) minaret, the
Paris Mosque forms a Moorish-style
enclave in the heart of the capital.

271

Discovered in 1870 during the building of Rue Monge, the ruins of the
Arènes de Lutèce (the ancient
name of Paris) have been conserved and its bleachers restored.

272 and 273
With its light-flooded glass and steel architecture, the Arab World Institute, built by Jean Nouvel in 1988, is a blend of tradition and modernity. The south façade of the building is imbued with the ancestral atmosphere of 240 Middle-Eastern-style meshrebeeyehs. The Institute stands by the Pont Sully, which connects it to the Île Saint-Louis and the right bank of the Seine.

274
The glass and steel Tour Zaman-sky rises in the center of the University of Paris VI: Pierre et Marie Curie, better known as the Jussieu Campus. The tower was built by Édouard Albert in 1971.

275
The Gare d'Austerlitz was inaugurated in 1840 and was extended 30 years later by Pierre-Louis Renaud.

276 and 277

Founded in the 17th century, the Salpetrière hospital has been extensively rebuilt and forms a large complex. Its imposing buildings, clustered
around a chapel with a Greek-cross plan, were merged with those of the
Nouvelle Pitié in 1964, when the hospital acquired its current name of
Pitié-Salpetrière.

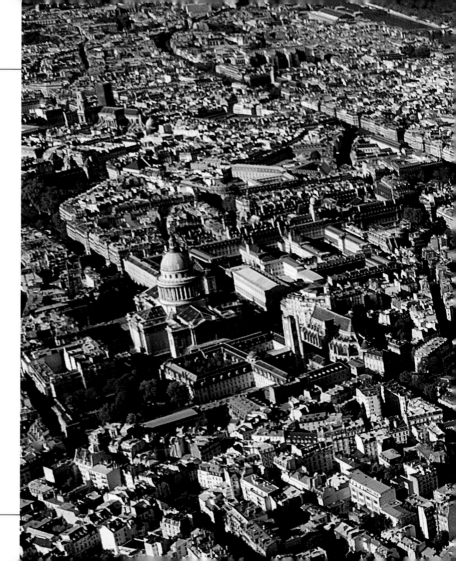

278-279

This aerial view, with the Latin Quarter on the left, reveals the extent of the area occupied by the huge Jussieu Campus.

280 and 281
The National Library of France (the François Mitterrand site) was built by Dominique Perrault in the Tolbiac quarter and opened to the public in 1996. Standing at the top of the great stairway, the esplanade is surrounded by four 259-foot (79 m) L-shaped towers, whose form recalls the shape of an open book.

282
The Joséphine Baker floating swimming pool can be reached from the Quai de la Gare. It was built by the architect Robert de Busni and "launched" in 2005.

283
Despite its appearance, the Bateau-Phare does not cruise the river, but is an old barge that has been converted into a restaurant.

284
Avenue de France, in the 13th *arrondissement*, overlooks the railway lines of the Gare d'Austerlitz.

285
Parisians have a penchant for nature and gardening, and are gradually transforming once neglected spaces, like these terraces on the banks of the Seine, into delightful hanging gardens.

THE RIVE DROITE:
LEGENDS AND DISCOVERIES

FLYING HIGH

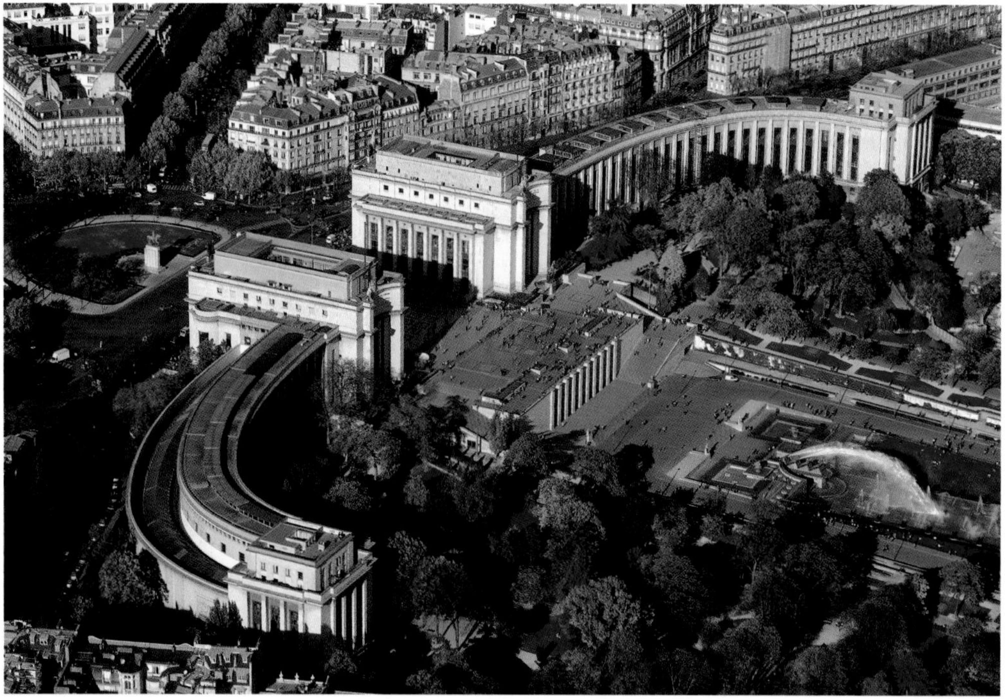

287
The low dome of the Paris Opéra (left). The Île aux Cygnes is an artificial island with a tree-lined walkway (right).

The Arc de Triomphe, which crowns the handsome vista of the Champs-Élysées, is one of Paris' most visited monuments. It was commissioned by Napoleon and celebrated by Victor Hugo in *Voix intérieures* ("Inner Voices"):

Toi dont la courbe au loin par le couchant dorée
S'emplit d'azur céleste, arche démesurée

(You, o enormous arch, whose curve
is filled with azure in the gilded gloaming)

Its construction took over 30 years to complete. Conceived in the style of the ancient triumphal arches, the Arc de Triomphe dominates the 12 avenues that are laid out to form a star. Hence the square's original name (Place de l'Étoile), which was subsequently changed to Place Charles de Gaulle. It was designed by Jean Chalgrin in 1806 and completed by Abel Blouet in 1836. The Arc de Triomphe is decorated with reliefs, friezes, sculptural groups and busts carved by the greatest artists of the period. The four inner faces are inscribed with the names of 174 battles and 700 military heroes. The arch stands 165 ft (50 m) tall and the view from the top, reached by 284 steps, is truly impressive, extending well beyond Neuilly.

The straight course of the Champs-Élysées has not been altered since 1828, but in 1994 the sidewalks were widened and Jean-Michel Wilmotte and Norman Foster modernized the street furnishings. Beyond the rotunda with its eye-catching flowerbeds, the Grand Palais and the Petit Palais on Avenue Winston Churchill (which leads to Pont Alexandre III), recall the splendor of the Universal Exposition of 1900. Designed

288
The Palais de Chaillot is formed by two pavilions with two curved wings, which overlook a large esplanade.

The Rive Droite:
Legends and Discoveries

by Charles Girault, the two buildings stand opposite each other, testifying to the creative flair of their builder. They are adorned with a plethora of colonnades, busts, statues and quadrigae; intricate floral, fruit and animal motifs; and a wide variety of tributes to French statuary art. Casts of Guillaume Coustou the Elder's *Horse Tamers* stand guard on either side of the far end of the Champs-Élysées where it meets the Place de la Concorde. The architecture of this famous royal square designed by Ange-Jacques Gabriel for Louis XV, was remodeled by Jacob Ignaz Hittorff following the erection of the Luxor Obelisk in 1836. The Egyptian monument rises in the center of the square and is flanked on both sides by imposing fountains – the Fountain of the Seas and the Fountain of the Rivers – which are both are the joint works of various artists. Surrounded by handsome streetlamps, rostral columns and statues, the northern side of the square is occupied by the Hôtel de la Marine and its identical twin, the Hôtel de Crillon, which is now a luxury hotel frequented by jet-setters from all over the world. Place François 1er is a tranquil haven in the Champs-Élysées quarter, surrounded by handsome mansions built at the end of the 19th century and adorned with a fountain by Gabriel Davioud that is dedicated to Jean Goujon.

The Rue du Faubourg Saint-Honoré is home to the Regency-style Palais de l'Élysée designed by Claude-Armand Mollet, which is now the official residence of the President of the French Republic. Its most famous occupant was undoubtedly Madame de Pompadour, who lived there in 1753. A monumental iron gate, known as the Grille du Coq (Rooster Gate) faces onto the Champs-Élysées, while the entrance on Faubourg Saint-Honoré is flanked by four Ionic columns and opens onto a circular courtyard. The palace's gardens have been landscaped, with woods and large flowerbeds surrounding a large fountain. On the other side of the quarter, the Neoclassical-style Madeleine

The Rive Droite:
Legends and Discoveries

church was begun in the mid-18th century and was not completed until almost a century later.

Two large department stores were also built in this quarter. Printemps, which opened in 1865, was rebuilt in the Art Nouveau style in 1881 by Paul Sibille following a fire. The nearby Galeries Lafayette (founded in 1893) was inaugurated in 1912 within a building with a Neo-Byzantine dome designed by Georges Chedanne and Ferdinand Chanut. These two stores are famous for their Christmas decorations. Their founders built them in a strategic position near the Gare Saint-Lazare, originally known as the Embarcadère de l'Ouest. The station was built between 1842 and 1853 by Alfred Armand and Eugène Flachant, and was inaugurated in 1867 by Napoleon III. It was extended and restored in 1936 and serves the Parisian suburbs.

The Paris Opéra is one of the largest opera houses in the world, covering an area of 118,404 square feet (36,090 square meters). It was designed in an ostenta-tious Baroque style by Charles Garnier and construction commenced in 1862. It was inaugurated 15 years later, in 1875. Its eclectic and sumptuous decoration required the skills of 73 sculptors (including Jean-Baptiste Carpeaux), 14 painters and 14 mosaicists.

The architect Alexandre-Théodore Brongniart died in 1813, before finishing the palace commissioned by Napoleon in 1807, and it was Etienne-Eloy Labarre who finally completed the Paris Bourse. The stock exchange stopped trading at the end of the 1990s and has been converted into a venue for exhibitions and seminars.

The quarter of La Trinité, situated next to that of Nouvelle Athènes, was long a district of bankers, whose offices were located near the Bourse. Several *Boulevard theatre* actresses also built charming houses in the area, many of which are now hidden behind tall façades and are visible only from the sky. La Trinité church, in Place d'Estienne

FLYING HIGH PARIS

The Palais des Congrès displays its daring architecture on the
edge of the Périphérique ring road, with a sloping façade
designed by Christian de Portzamparc.

d'Orves at the end of Rue Lafayette, is built in the Second Empire architectural style.

Higher up, around Place Saint-Georges, several mansions have been conserved and transformed into libraries or museums. Prime examples are the Fondation Dosne-Thiers, the house of Gustave Moreau and that of the sculptor Ary Scheffer. The Parc Monceau covers an area of over 915,000 square feet (278,900 square meters). It became a public park in 1861 and is adorned with many statues and spectacular trees. It is one of the largest parks in Paris and a meeting place for local residents and the members of the Russian community who frequent the Saint-Alexandre-Nevski Cathedral. The cathedral was also completed in 1861 and was designed in the style of the Church of the Ascension in Kolomenskoye, by the Russian architects Kouzmine and Strohm. The church of Saint-Augustin, on the other hand, was built in the Neo-Byzantine style and was an important part of Baron Haussmann's rebuilding scheme. Place des Ternes is a large square located between the 8th and 17th *arrondissements*, opposite the Arc de Triomphe and near the quiet Place Saint-Ferdinand.

The elegant buildings of the 16th *arrondissement* begin in the Place du Trocadéro. The square is dominated by the Palais de Chaillot, which houses the Musée National de la Marine and the Musée de l'Homme. This quiet residential quarter is also home to the Musée Guimet, a temple of Asian art, and the Palais de Tokyo, with its collection of contemporary art. Continuing beyond the quays along the Seine, the enormous Maison de Radio France, inaugurated in 1963, covers an area of over one million square feet (304,800 square meters) and houses the offices of the French radio company. Beyond Porte Maillot, the *arrondissement* also includes the Bois de Boulogne. This 2090-acre park is the ideal spot for pleasant strolls, and is home to a zoo, a rose garden, large lakes with rowboats, two racecourses and the site of the former Racing Club.

294 and 295
These two photographs taken at different times of day show the Arc de
Triomphe and the streets that radiate out from it.

296 and 297
At 165 feet (49 m) high, 148 feet (45 m) wide and 72 feet (22 m) deep,
the Arc de Triomphe, in Place du Général de Gaulle, is much larger
than the ancient triumphal arches on which it was modeled. The 450-
foot (137 m) relief that surrounds it depicts the departure and return of
the French armies.

298

The Arc de Triomphe was commissioned by Napoleon to dominate the vista of the Champs-Élysées and offers visitors spectacular views of Paris.

299

The Tomb of the Unknown Soldier, whose flame is rekindled every evening, was placed under the central arch in 1929. It holds the remains of an anonymous soldier who died in the Battle of Verdun.

300
Viewed from here, the Champs-Élysées deserves its moniker of *La plus belle avenue du monde* ("The most beautiful avenue in the world").

301
The Seine flows from the Debilly footbridge to Pont Alexandre III. Bateaux
Mouches can be seen moored on the left of the photograph, with the
Grand Palais beyond.

302 and 303
The Champs-Élysées is 230 feet (70 m) wide and 1.25 miles (2 km) long. It is one of the one of the most important thoroughfares in Paris. Viewed from above, the Historical Axis extends in a straight line as far as the eye can see, from Place de la Concorde to La Défense.

304
With the Tuileries Gardens in the background, the lower part of the Champs-Élysées and Place de la Concorde are shrouded in white mist.

305
Traffic in the Champs-Élysées is hectic on both the road and the sidewalks, which are always packed with pedestrians.

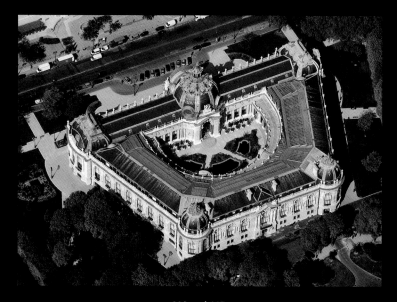

306 and 307
The main façade of the trapezoidal Petit Palais is adorned with an
imposing portico surmounted by a cupola. The building is framed by
the lush green gardens of the Champs-Élysées.

308

The Grand Palais stands opposite the Petit Palais, both of which were built for the Universal Exposition of 1900. In 1937 they were joined by the Palais de la Dé- couverte, erected for the International Ex- position of Art and Technology.

309

The Grand Palais is an emblem of Belle Époque architecture. The building is 787 feet (240 m) long and 144 feet (44 m) tall and features a huge triple portal and a façade dominated by a pair of quadrigae by Georges Récipon.

310-311

The restoration of the glass ceiling of the Grand Palais required several years and 700 original pieces.

312-313
Place François 1er is lined with handsome buildings, such as the Hôtel de Vilgruy, built by Henri Labrouste, the architect of the Sainte-Geneviève Library, in 1865.

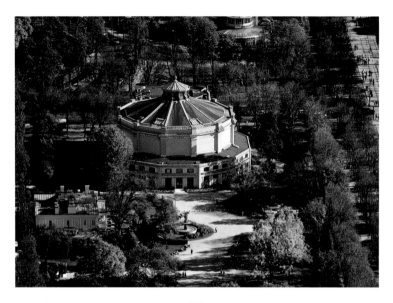

314
The handsome Théâtre Marigny, in the gardens of the Champs-Élysées,
was opened in 1835 and rebuilt by Charles Garnier in 1880.

315
The church of Saint-Pierre de Chaillot (1938), brings a geometric note to
the Avenue Marceau with its handsome late-19th-century buildings.

316
The city's municipal gardeners do a magnificent job, planting the flowerbeds of the rotunda of the Champs-Élysées with Christmas trees dusted with artificial snow in November.

317
At sunset, the Arc de Triomphe stands out clearly from the surrounding buildings.

318 and 319
Unlike other royal squares, the Place de la Concorde is open to the surrounding landscape. The 75-foot (23 m) obelisk at its center is crowned by a gilded pyramidion and flanked by two monumental fountains.

320-321
The Élysée Palace in Rue du Faubourg Saint-Honoré has been the official residence of the President of the French Republic since 1873. In 1991 the gardens were re-arranged and fountains added.

322-323
This quarter, which showcases the Neoclassical Madeleine church, is served by wide avenues that lead to the Paris Opéra in one direction and Place de la Concorde in the other and is home to important banks and luxury stores.

324 and 325

The Madeleine church, consecrated in 1845, was modeled on a Greek
temple and built in several stages over almost a century. Its pediment,
visible on the right in the soft winter light, is adorned with a relief of the
Last Judgment by Philippe-Henri Lemaire.

326 and 327
Avenue Marceau is an elegant thoroughfare that extends from Place de l'Etoile to Place de l'Alma. The solidity of the church of Saint-Pierre de Chaillot, built by Emile Bois, is accentuated by the use of concrete as a building material.

328 and 329
Viewed from both the front and the back, the Paris Opéra is an imposing structure that rises above the other buildings of the quarter. Circular pavilions with domes painted the same pale green as that of the main building have been added to either side.

330-331
Situated at the end of Avenue de l'Opéra, the building exemplifies the Napoleon III style and fits in perfectly with the surrounding structures built by Baron Haussmann.

332
Five small wooden boxes can be seen on the roof of the Opéra, topped with a pale green dome. They are beehives belonging a retired prop man, who gathers delicious and highly sought-after honey from them.

334 and 335
The façade is adorned with the busts of famous musicians, while the roof
is surmounted with two gilded sculptural groups of *Poetry* and *Harmony*.

336 and 337
Boulevard Haussmann joins Avenue de Friedland at the junction of Boulevard des Italiens and Boulevard Montmartre. It is home to two famous department stores: Printemps and the Galeries Lafayette. The former was founded in 1865, but its stained-glass cupola was built by the master glazier Eugéne Brière in 1923.

338
The roof of this building in Rue de la Michodière has a circular skylight.

339
Formerly the Paris Bourse, Palais Brongniart is named after the architect who began its construction in 1807. The two wings, added in 1923, give the building its current cross-shaped plan.

340
The Gare Saint-Lazare lies between Rue de Rome and Rue d'Amsterdam and is entered from the Cour de Rome.

341
Nearby, Place de l'Europe is situated on a viaduct, overlooking the railway tracks below.

342 and 343
Each year 85 million passengers frequent the 27 platforms of the Gare
Saint-Lazare. The station has been rebuilt several times since 1837 and is
one of Paris' six great railway terminuses.

344

The Nouvelle Athènes quarter was commenced in 1830. Its name refers to the classical inspiration of the architects of the period. It is home to charming old-fashioned apartment blocks and little mansions, surrounded by delightful gardens. Place Saint-Georges stands in the center of the quarter.

346-347
The charm of Place Saint-Georges, adorned with a statue of Paul Gavarni by Denys Puech erected in 1904, is underscored by the Hôtel Thiers, now the headquarters of the Fondation Dosne-Thiers.

348 and 349
La Trinité church, overlooking Place d'Estienne d'Orves, was built by Théodore Ballu between 1861 and 1867. It is distinguished by a tall bell tower that rises above a three-arched portico and a plethora of sculptural groups.

350 and 351

The church of Notre-Dame-de-Lorette, built by Louis-Hippolyte Lebas between 1823 and 1836, is situated on the busy Rue de Châteaudun. Its architecture is inspired by the plan of Santa Maria Maggiore in Rome.

352 and 353
The church of Saint-Augustin, standing in the square of the same name at the junction of Boulevard Malesherbes and Boulevard Haussmann, was built by Victor Baltard between 1860 and 1871. It is situated in the Saint-Lazare district, where many houses have now been converted into offices.

354

Rue Daru is a meeting place for Paris' Russian community and home to the Saint-Alexandre-Nevski Cathedral. The building's five turrets are topped with onion domes featuring the eight-armed Eastern Orthodox cross.

355

The Hôtel Salomon de Rothschild was built by Léon Ohnet in 1874 to house the art collection of the baron after whom it is named. It is now home to the Fondation Nationale des Arts Graphiques Plastiques.

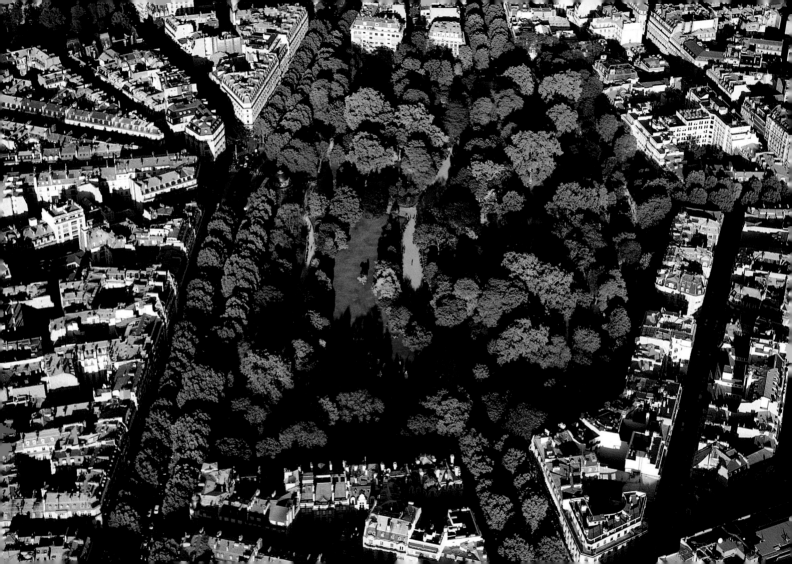

356 and 357
The Parc Monceau measures over half a mile (1 km) around and is situated in the heart of the 8th *arrondissement*. It has four entrances, with the main one on Boulevard de Courcelles.

358

After entering the gate by Gabriel Davioud, visitors can admire the Rotonde de Chartres by Claude Nicolas Ledoux.

359

On the far left of the photograph on the right, lies the mansion of Count Moïse de Camondo, with a garden opening onto Parc Monceau. It was built in the 18th century by René Sergent.

360
One of the tall buildings framing Place des Ternes conceals a circular inner courtyard with a garden.

361
The spire-topped dome of the former Magasins Réunis, built in 1912, reaches towards the sky at the junction between Avenue MacMahon and Avenue des Ternes.

362-363
The tree-shaded Place des Ternes, at the meeting point of Avenue de Wagram, Boulevard de Courcelles, Rue du Faubourg Saint-Honoré and Avenue des Ternes is the site of one of Paris' few remaining flower markets.

364
Not far from Place des Ternes, Place Saint-Ferdinand is situated at the junction of Rue Brunel and Rue Saint-Ferdinand. A monument to Léon Serpollet by Jean Boucher stands in its center.

365
Avenue de Friedland stretches from Rue de Washington and Rue Saint-Honoré to Place Charles de Gaulle. It is home to grand hotels and embassies, as well as the Paris Chamber of Commerce, whose building occupies a corner plot.

FLYING HIGH PARIS

366
The Trocadéro quarter is dominated by the Palais de Chaillot, whose huge wings extend along the Seine, opposite the Tour Eiffel and the Champ de Mars.

368 and 369

Viewed from Place Trocadéro, the two central pavilions of Palais de Chaillot are separated by the Esplanade des Droits de l'Homme. The palace's wings conceal a 23-acre landscaped garden.

370
The esplanade is a magnet for tourists, who flock there to admire the view.

371
The Musée Guimet, recently restored by Henri and Bruno Gaudin, is located in Place d'Iéna, on the corner between Rue d'Iéna and Rue Boissière. The offices of the Western European Union (WEU) rise opposite it, in Avenue d'Iéna.

372 and 373
Bateaux Mouches can be boarded at Port de la Conférence, beneath
Pont de l'Alma. Further along the Seine, the boats pass beneath the De-
billy footbridge.

374 and 375
With the Pont Mirabeau in the foreground, Bartholdi's replica of the
Statue of Liberty, inaugurated in 1889, resembles a figurehead on the
tip of the 2,900-foot-long (890 m) Île aux Cygnes.

376 and 377

The Maison de Radio France, on the Quai du Président Kennedy, was designed by Henry Bernard in 1963. The circular aluminum-clad building is 1640 feet (500 m) across and 121 feet (37 m) tall, with a 226-foot (68 m) central tower.

378
The glass and metal Residence Passy-Kennedy overlooks the Seine near the Maison de Radio France.

379 left
The enormous Palais de Tokyo is visible to the left of the Debilly footbridge.

379 right
This view shows three of Paris' bridges: Pont de la Concorde, Pont Alexandre III and Ponte des Invalides.

380-381
The Palais de Tokyo is situated between Avenue du Président-Wilson
and Avenue de New York. It was
built for the International Exposition of Art and Technology in 1937.

382
Opposite the Palais de Tokyo, the Palais Galliera, built by Léon Ginain between 1878 and 1894, houses the Musée de Mode et du Costume.

383
The Palais de Tokyo is home to both the Musée d'Art Moderne and the
Site de Création Contemporaine, rebuilt by Anne Lacaton and Jean-
Philippe Vassal in 2002.

384

Porte Maillot is an important junction on the western edge of Paris, between the city's Avenue de la Grande-Armée and Neuilly's Avenue Charles-de-Gaulle. It stands above the Périphérique ring road.

385

Place de la Porte Maillot, located between the Arc de Triomphe and La Défense, is adorned with an oval 173,500-square-foot (16,125 sq m) garden, built in 1974.

386

Rue Henri-Martin, stretching from the Trocadéro to Rue de Franqueville, is shaded by clusters of trees. It is one of the most elegant streets of the 16th *arrondissement*.

387

The Ranelagh quarter, near the Bois de Boulogne, is one of the most spacious in Paris and is home to private villages and houses with little gardens.

388 and 389
Boulevard Suchet extends from Place de la Colombie to Porte d'An-
teuil. It is overlooked by mansions and huge buildings, some of which
are adorned with splendid hanging gardens.

390

Near Place de la Porte d'Auteuil, twin buildings separated by a shady courtyard open on one side onto Boulevard Suchet and on the other onto the Auteuil Racecourse.

391

Lying between Rue Michel-Ange and Rue Boileau, like a village in the Auteuil quarter, Hameau Boileau is an expanse of greenery dotted with houses, which look more like holiday homes than Parisian residences.

392

Inaugurated in 1897 and renovated in 1932, the futuristic third Parc des Princes stadium was designed by Roger Taillebert in 1972. It is able to hold almost 44,000 spectators.

393

The land that belonged to the exclusive Racing Club de France until 2006 lies along the shore of the Lower Lake in the in the Bois de Boulogne. Its fine swimming pool and 48 tennis courts make it a very popular spot.

394 and 395

In the heart of the Bois de Boulogne, on the edge of Neuilly, the 47-acre Jardin d'Acclimatation was founded in 1860 as the world's first leisure park. These legendary gardens, which have delighted generations of children, have been given a new lease of life by the artist Hippolyte Romain, who has been the artistic director for the past ten years.

396
The 2090-acre Bois de Boulogne still reserves several surprises, particularly the Longchamp Racecourse, which covers an area of 141 acres along the Route des Tribunes.

397
The Roland Garros stadium, on the edge of the Bois de Boulogne, was built in 1928 for the Davis Cup. Each year its 24 courts host the French Open Grand Slam tennis tournament.

398 and 399
The outdoor Olympic-size swimming pool of the former Racing Club,
is situated in the Pré Catalan and is frequented by its privileged
members in summer.

400

Place des Etats-Unis is a green oasis in the 16th *arrondissement,* surrounded by mansions that once belonged to celebrities. The gardens in its center are a familiar spot for the children of this quarter.

401

With its cascade basins and powerful jets of water, the Fontaine de Varsovie in the Trocadéro Gardens is an endless source of delight.

THE INNER CITY AND THE SUBURBS:
A MOVING, EXPANDING CITY

FLYING HIGH

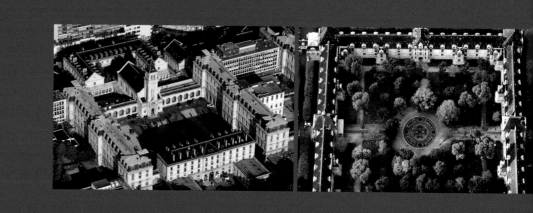

FLYING HIGH PARIS

403

The Hôpital Saint-Louis in the 10th *arrondissement* and the Hôpital Tenon in the
20th both boast a square garden similar to that of a cloister.

In addition to Paris' fantastic tourist attractions in the central and also the slightly further outlying areas (e.g. Montmartre), the adjoining suburbs also offer interesting contemporary sites. Likewise, several of the less well-frequented arrondissements, which are now business districts, are home to some handsome, long-forgotten buildings that have known better days. Indeed, fashions change, but stone and steel masterpieces remain. Hospitals, for example, fired the imaginations of many architects and hygienists between the late-18th and early-19th centuries. This is confirmed by the elaborate architecture and relaxing gardens of the Hôpital Saint-Louis and Hôpital Lariboisière in the 10th arrondissement and also that of the Hôpital Tenon in the 20th *arrondissement*. Churches have always reflected the tastes of their architects. Examples include Saint-Lambert and Saint-Ambroise, built in the Romanesque Revival style; Saint-Laurent, rebuilt in several stages during the 15th century; the bizarre Saint-Jean-de-Montmartre, built from reinforced concrete and studded with colored cabochon stones; Notre-Dame-de-la-Croix; and of course, the most famous duo of all, Notre-Dame and the Sacré-Cœur. Railway stations have also provided food for thought for the city's planners. The Gare du Nord and the Gare de l'Est in the 10th *arrondissement* were designed by Jacques

404

The vineyard, the garden of the little museum and the Jardin Sauvage
Saint-Vincent form a large green area with gazebos in Montmartre.

The Inner City and the Suburbs:
A Moving, Expanding City

Ignace Hittorff,, who gave them unusually large windows, while the Belle Époque atmosphere of the 12th *arrondissement* inspired Marius Toudoire's Gare de Lyon. The Bercy district was once home to Paris' wine market and is situated opposite the Gare de Lyon. It has undergone radical change since the 1970s, acquiring a spectacular panorama marked by the Palais Omnisports, the Ministry of Finances and the recently refurbished Parc de Bercy. The 13th *arrondissement* is off the beaten tourist track. This old working-class district is home to the Manufacture des Gobelins tapestry factory, founded in 1664. The original 17th-century buildings are still intact behind an early 20th-century façade. Place d'Italie is the heart of the quarter and is a transit point between Paris and the Périphérique ring road, Montparnasse Station and the Rive Droite. The 15th *arrondissement* is home to the 35-acre Parc André Citroën, which is little known to both tourists and Parisians alike. Opened in 1992, the park boasts a varied selection of gardens, greenhouses, fountains and the world's largest hot air balloon, operated by the Eutelsat company. This allows groups of 12 to 20 visitors to admire the Parisian skyline from a new angle. The nearby, and very commercial, Rue Saint-Charles heralds the buildings of the Front-de-Seine, with its amazing, ultra-modern urban landscape. The quarter, also known as Beaugrenelle, is comprised of a series of 330-foot (100 m) towers that were built during the 1970s. The Square Saint-Lambert park is full of surprises. The large symmetrical lawns, a pool and many different species of trees cover an area of 223,300 square feet (68,062 square meters) that is also dotted with sculptures by artists including René Paris and Victor Reter. Parc Georges-Brassens was inaugurated in 1982 and covers almost 20 acres. A secondhand-book market is held beneath a large canopy on weekends. The entrance to the

The Inner City and the Suburbs:
A Moving, Expanding City

park is marked by a pair of bulls sculpted by Auguste Cain in 1878, reminding visitors that it was formerly the site of Paris' cattle market.

Montmartre is a village within the city, to the extent that its inhabitants say that they are, "going to Paris" when they visit the city center. The buildings of the quarter are listed, and consequently its appearance has changed little since the days when the narrow, winding streets were frequented by Picasso, Toulouse-Lautrec and other great artists.

The name Montmartre immediately brings to mind the Sacré-Cœur Basilica, which dominates the city. Other landmarks include the Place du Tertre, which was frequented by painters and the Moulin de la Galette windmill. Avenue Junot, whose artists' studios have been converted into homes; the romantic Château-des-Brouillards; the Lapin Agile cabaret; Rue Cortot, with its elegant local museum and the vineyard, whose very small annual production is

highly sought after by Parisians and wine collectors finish off a very prestigious list. Many of the little houses conceal pretty gardens, lovingly tended by their owners.

In recent years a former industrial quarter of factories, sawmills and garages has become one of the most fashionable districts of Paris: the Canal Saint-Martin, which extends for almost 3 miles (5 km) between the Bassin de la Villette to the Port de l'Arsenal among the newly-restored buildings.

The humble workshops with their interesting architecture have been converted into magnificent lofts overlooking the canal. On the edge of the Bassin, by the Parc de la Villette and La Géode, Claude Nicolas Ledoux's Rotonde de la Villette is one of the last remaining traces of Paris' old customs houses, along with one in Place de la Nation. The Neoclassical building creates an interesting contrast with the housing projects of Avenue de Flandre that were built

FLYING HIGH PARIS

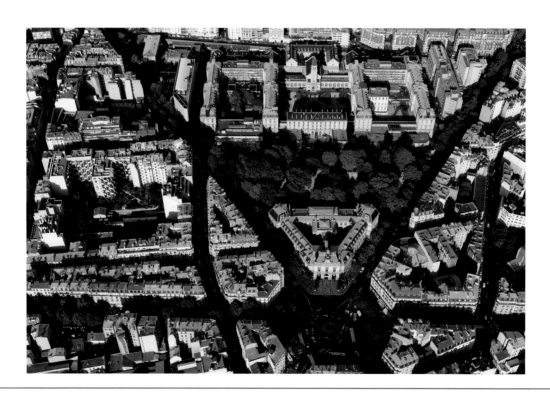

408
The Hôpital Tenon, with its courtyard and chapel, can be
glimpsed behind the Place Gambetta and its triangular city hall.

during the 1980s. This thoroughfare leads to the Parc de la Villette, which covers an area of 136 acres, making it the largest park in Paris. It is home to the Cité des Sciences et de l'Industrie, and was built by several different architects, commencing in 1985.

It includes such varied buildings as La Géode; the Grande Halle de La Villette, a huge covered market whose architecture echoes the glass and iron structures of the 19th century; Le Zénith, with its inflatable roof; the Cité de la Musique and a whole series of gardens.

The Stade de France stadium was built in 1995 on a former industrial site in the northern suburb of Saint-Denis by Michel Macary, Aymeric Zubléna, Michel Régembal and Claude Costantini. It is notable for its size and construction techniques, but also for its mobile oval roof, which moves 138 feet (42 m) above the pitch. A mile west of Paris, the business district of La Défense sums up the technical progress and daringness of contemporary architecture. Here the dreary, old-fashioned suburban houses of the Hauts-de-Seine quarter have been demolished and the road network redesigned to reduce congestion for traffic entering the city. Towers have been built, connected by suspended walkways that are adorned with art works and pretty corners, replacing the traditional sidewalks. The Arche de la Défense opens onto Paris on one side and the future on the other. It was designed by Johann Otto von Spreckelsen and built on the city's Axe Historique, at the opposite end to the Louvre. It represents the link between the Paris of the Enlightenment and that of the increasingly futuristic present.

410
The sweeping lawns and clipped hornbeams of the Parc André Citroën make it look more like an American campus rather than a Parisian park.

411
Rue Saint-Charles, in the business district of the 15th *arrondissement*, stretches for 1.25 miles (2 km) from Boulevard de Grenelle to Rue Leblanc.

412 and 413

Two buildings typical of the architecture of the 1960s and 1970s face
each other across the Seine: the
Maison de Radio France and the
towers of the Beaugrenelle quarter,
dominated by the Tour Paris Côté
Seine.

FLYING HIGH PARIS

415
The Square Saint-Lambert park was laid out in 1933 and blends well with the surrounding buildings dating from the same period.

416
The handsome brick and stone buildings between Boulevard Pasteur and Rue Brown-Sequard form an impeccable rectangle framed by trees.

417
This well-proportioned zinc-roofed block is situated in the 14th *arrondissement*.

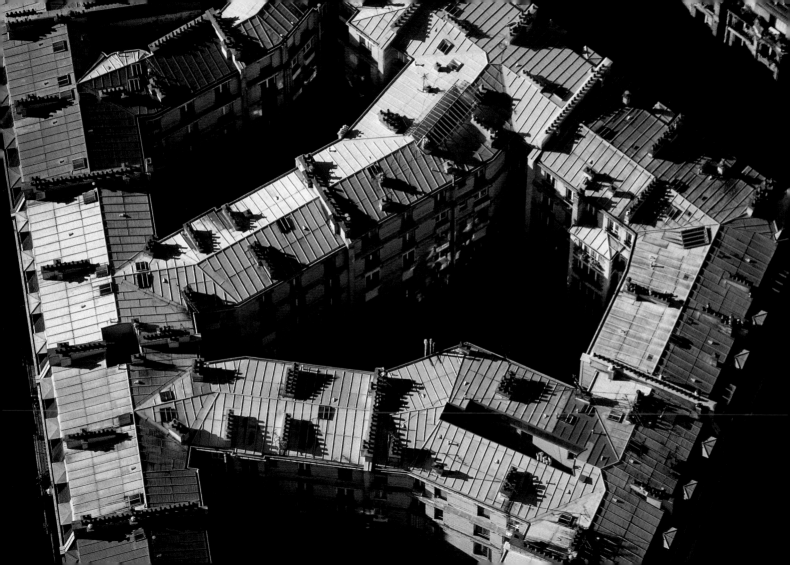

418
The Parc Georges Brassens is crisscrossed with paths, which also wind through its rose and herb gardens.

419
Boulevard Jourdan is flanked on the right by the Parc Montsouris and on the left by the irregular buildings of the Cité Internationale Universitaire de Paris.

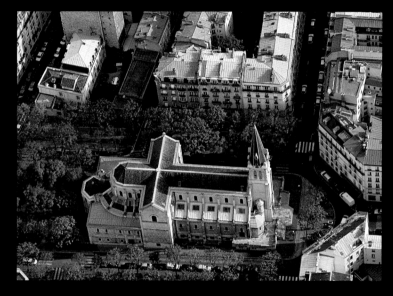

420

The center of Place d'Italie, in the 13th *arrondissement,* is home to a garden with a pool. A monument commemorates the Tunisian and Italian campaigns of Marshal Juin.

421

The handsome church of Saint-Lambert de Vaugirard was built in the Romanesque Revival style at the end of the 19th century.

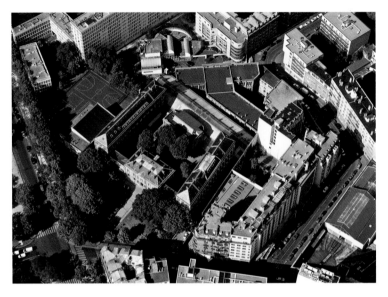

422
The tree-shaded courtyard of the École Estienne near Place d'Italie is
hidden behind a series of buildings.

423
The Manufacture des Gobelins tapestry factory has been part of the Mo-
bilier National since 1937 and comprises several buildings dating from
the 17th century and a façade built by Jean-Camille Formigé in 1914.

424-425
The soft light of an autumn evening colors the Vincennes zoo with shades of red. The concrete Grand Rocher can be clearly seen, with the suburb of Saint-Mandé on the left, while Daumesnil Lake is visible in the foreground.

426
The Porte Dorée, which formerly housed the Musée des Arts d'Afrique et d'Océanie, is a reinforced concrete building built in the Neoclassical style by Albert Laprade and Léon Jaussely for the 1931 Colonial Exhibition.

427
The Bois de Vincennes has several sports venues, including a racecourse and tennis courts.

428 and 429

Place de la Nation is one of Paris' largest squares. It measures 827 feet (252 m) across and has a monumental statue by Aimé-Jules Dalou in the center. The twin Doric columns of the Barrière du Trône and the pavilions of the customs house designed by Claude-Nicolas Ledouz in 1788 are still visible on the Cours de Vincennes side.

430-431
The Gare de Lyon was built by Marius Toudoire in 1899 and enlarged in 1927. The station opens onto Place Louis-Armand on Boulevard Diderot, extending from Quai de la Rapée to Place de la Nation.

432

Seen from above, the empty railway tracks branching out from Gare de Lyon look as though they lead nowhere.

433

The station is characterized by a 220-foot (67 m) square tower known as the Tour de l'Horloge, which is topped with a zinc dome. Each of the four sides of the tower has a clock face measuring 21 feet (6.5 m) across.

434
Between Pont de Bercy and Pont d'Austerlitz and the tip of the Île Saint-Louis, the Seine is crossed by Pont Charles de Gaulle, the Viaduc du Métro and the Viaduc d'Austerlitz Bercy.

435
The Palais Omnisports de Paris-Bercy was built by architects Michel Andrault and Pierre Parat in 1984 on the site of the former Grand Bercy wine warehouses.

436

Parc de Bercy was laid out by the architects Madeleine Ferrand, Jean-Pierre Feugas, Bernard Leroy and Bernard Huet, and the landscape gardeners Ian Le Caisne and Philippe Raguin between 1993 and 1997. It was inaugurated in 2000 and is home to the Jardin Yitzhak Rabin, named after the late Israeli prime minister.

437

The impressive building of the Ministry of Finances, which straddles the Quai de la Râpée to reach down to the Seine, was designed by Paul Chemetov and Borja Huidobro in 1989.

438 and 439
The Bastille district is dominated by two important historical sites: Place de la Bastille and Place des Vosges, which can be seen in the top left of the photograph. Several important thoroughfares run through the quarter, including the tree-lined Boulevard Beaumarchais, which connects Place de la Bastille with Boulevard des Filles du Calvaire. The July Column, topped with the famous Génie de la Liberté, rises in the center of the square.

440

The Promenade Plantée, running from Place de la Bastille to the Bois de Vincennes, is an elevated park designed by Philippe Mathieux and Jacques Vergely.

441

Tourist boats sail in and out of the Paris Arsenal port, with the July Column in the background.

442 and 443

The Porte Saint-Denis and Porte Saint-Martin are triumphal arches, commissioned by Louis XIV. They stand at the beginning of the streets after which they are named.

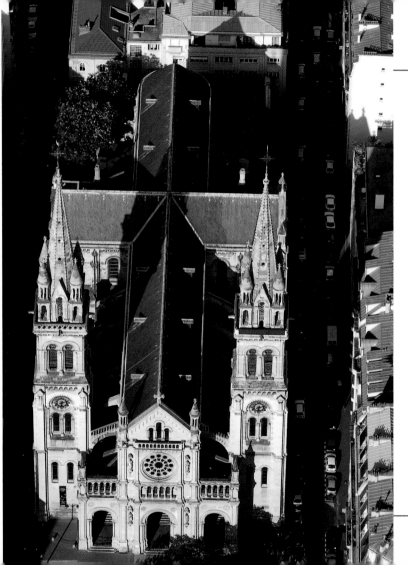

444

The church of Saint-Ambroise, on Boulevard Voltaire in the 11th *arrondissement*, was built in the Romanesque Revival style by Théodore Ballu.

445

Square Maurice Gardette was opened to the public in 1872 and is adorned with majestic trees and beautiful flowerbeds. In summer the Napoléon III bandstand offers live music and there are play areas for children.

446
The Place de la République lies between the 3rd, 10th and 11th *arrondissements*. It was designed by Baron Haussman in 1862 as part of his grandiose urban rebuilding scheme. In 1883 the center was adorned with a bronze statue entitled *La République* by the Morice brothers.

447
The Lycée Voltaire, between Avenue de la République and Boulevard de Ménilmontant, was built by Eugène Train and inaugurated in 1890.

448
The architect used a metal framework for the glass roofs of the Gare de l'Est, built in 1850.

449
Built by Jacques-Ignace Hittorf between 1861 and 1865, the Gare du Nord was greatly admired for the lightness of its windows and its monumental façade inspired by the architecture of ancient Roman baths.

450
The church of Saint-Laurent, on Boulevard Magenta, was founded in 1429 and rebuilt several times up until 1870.

451
The Jardin Villemin was laid out in 1977 in the style of a classic 19th-century garden. It occupies an area of five acres between the Convent of the Recollects and the Canal Saint-Martin.

452-453
The monument to Marshal Moncey, built by Amédée Doublemard in 1869, stands in the center of Place Clichy, at the junction of Rue Caulaincourt and Boulevard de Clichy.

454
Bordering on the Boulevard de Clichy and Place Blanche (in the lower part of the photograph) the buildings of lower Montmartre surround the Montmartre cemetery on the left.

455
Rue Moncey is home to a pretty garden of the same name. It can be reached by taking Rue de Cliché from Place Clichy.

456

Place Pigalle lies between the 9th and 18th *arrondissements* and separates Boulevard de Cliché from Boulevard de Rochechouart.

457

Place Blanche is home to one of the most famous cabarets in the world: the Moulin Rouge. Its sails, designed by Adolphe Willette have been turn-

458-459

The dazzling white Sacré-Cœur Basilica dominates Paris from the summit of Butte Montmartre. The building in the Romano-Byzantine-style was commenced in 1876 and completed in 1914.

460

Construction of the 135,000-square-foot (12,500 sq m) basilica was commenced by Paul Abadie, but six other architects were needed to complete it.

461

The huge basilica, with a Greek cross plan, is 328 feet (100 m) long and 164 feet (50 m) wide. The central dome, which rises 262 feet (80 m), is surmounted by a lantern.

462
The central dome of the basilica is surrounded by four smaller oval ones.

463
The imposing entrance is flanked
by two equestrian statues of Joan
of Arc and Saint Louis by Lefebvre.

464 and 465
The Square Willette at the foot of the basilica was laid out by Formigé, who built terraces on the hillside descending to Place
Saint-Pierre.

466
Montmartre is full of little bistros, like this one in Place Saint-Pierre, opposite the gardens of the basilica.

467
Place du Tertre, in Montmartre, is a favorite tourist spot. It is surrounded with charming houses, the first of which was built in 1790.

468

The rooftops between Rue Simart, Rue Marcadet and Rue Eugène Sue form an eye-catching geometric pattern.

469

Several modest-looking buildings between Rue Lepic and Rue Norvins conceal beautiful gardens.

470
This aerial view extending from the Saint-Vincent cemetery to Avenue Junot reveals the number and extent of hidden walled gardens, which constitute the secret lungs of Montmartre.

471
Saint-Jean-de-Montmartre in Place des Abbesses was the first reinforced concrete church in France, built by Anatole de Baudot in 1900.

472-473
Many fine houses with gardens have been built between the Saint-Vincent cemetery, the vineyard and the Jardin Sauvage.

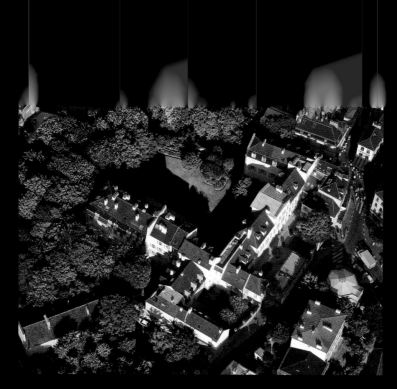

474

Rue Norvins winds between the houses and gardens of the upper part of Montmartre.

475

The Moulin de la Galette, restored in 1978, is one of the two surviving windmills of Montmartre's original twelve.

476
Avenue de Flandre in the 19th *arrondissement* connects Place de Stalingrad with Avenue Corentin-Carriou.

477
The huge Place des Fêtes with its two enormous towers was restored during the 1990s. The brick roofs of the Mouzaïa district are visible in the top left of the photograph.

478 and 479
The Parc des Buttes-Chaumont occupies an area of 62 acres and was inaugurated in 1867. It is home to a five-acre artificial lake featuring an island adorned with a temple and a grotto.

480
The round temple built on the island was designed by Gabriel Davioud in 1869 and is modeled on the Italian Temple of the Sybil, after which it is named.

481
The bandstand of the Parc des Buttes-Chaumont is situated on one of the lawns where visitors relax.

482

The city hall of the 19th *arrondissement* is situated in Place Armand Carrel, opposite the Parc des Buttes-Chaumont. It was built by Gabriel Davioud and Jules Bourdais between 1876 and 1878.

483

This aerial view reveals the perfect tree-edged semicircle formed by the buildings in Rue Simon Bolivar, between the Parc des Buttes-Chaumont and the Stalingrad district.

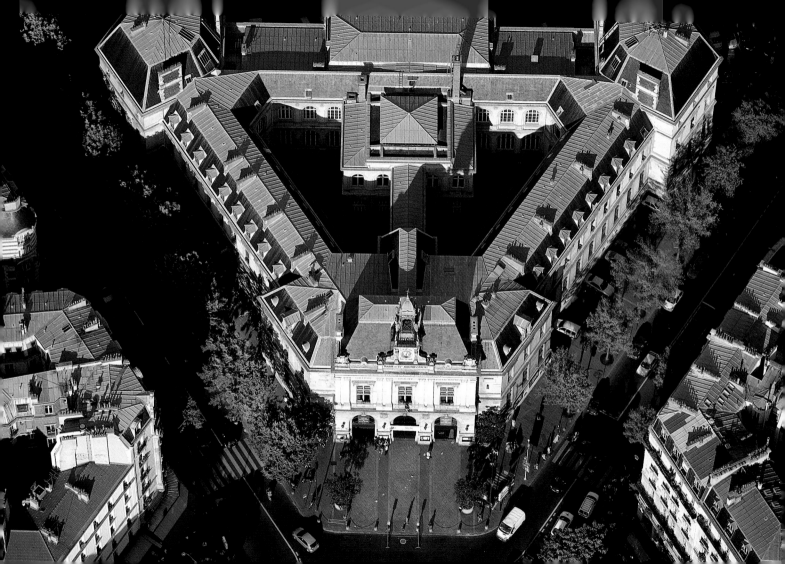

484

The city hall of the 20th *arrondissement*, in Place Gambetta, was built by Claude-Augustin Salleron between 1887 and 1897.

485

The chapel of the Hôpital Tenon is set in quiet and well-manicured grounds and is part of the late-19th-century complex.

486 and 487

The Père-Lachaise Cemetery attracts many tourists. It covers an area of 118 acres and is planted with 12,000 trees. Many of the tombs of its 97 burial sections are adorned with fanciful sculptures. The crematorium, built in 1886 by Formigé, stands in the center of the columbarium.

488
The church of Notre-Dame-de-la-Croix in Ménilmontant was commenced in 1863 and has a 256-foot (78 m) bell tower.

489
The Parc de Belleville was inaugurated in 1988 and boasts extensive lawns, a cascade fountain, children's play areas and flowerbeds. It is surrounded by the Rue de Couronnes.

490 and 491
The brick and stone Hôpital Saint-Louis was built by Claude Vellefaux between 1607 and 1611. It forms a well-proportioned quadrilateral around a
large shady courtyard.

492

Shown here with Boulevard Macdonald in the foreground, the Canal Saint-Denis is navigable for about four miles.

493

The Mouzaïa district lies below Place des Fêtes and is formed by pretty little houses adorned with flowers which were built by Paul Fouquiau at the turn of the 20th century.

494 and 495
The buildings of the Cité des Sciences et de l'Industrie, dedicated to science, technology and industry, were built by Adrien Fainsilber, while the Cité de la Musique was designed by Christian de Portzamparc.

496
Le Zénith is a concert venue, built by Philippe Chaix and Jean-Paul Morel in 1983, which can accommodate over 6000 spectators.

497
The Cité de la Musique was built by Christian de Portzamparc between 1992 and 1994.

498 and 499
La Géode, situated behind the Cité des Sciences et de l'Industrie and
the Cité de la Musique, is a huge sphere measuring 118 feet (36 m)
across. It was built by Adrien Fainsilber using polished stainless steel,
which reflects the light. It was inaugurated in 1985.

500 and 501

Next to the Périphérique ring road around the Porte de Montreuil, the multicolored stalls of the Montreuil Flea Market, founded in 1860, offer a kaleidoscope of wares.

502
Near the Porte de Bagnolet junction, Les Mercuriales, otherwise known as the Tour Levant and Tour Ponant, were built by Serge Lana between 1975 and 1977 as part of an urban planning scheme that was never completed.

503
The Périphérique ring road runs past the oval Bercy II shopping center in the 12th *arrondissement*.

FLYING HIGH PARIS

505
The business district of La Défense was conceived by the city planners Auzelle, Dufau and Guitton at the beginning of the 1960s. It now covers an area of 395 acres.

506 and 507
On the esplanade, pedestrians walk through the enormous legs of
Alexander Calder's *L'Araignée Rouge* ("Red Spider"), erected in 1976.

508 and 509

Towards the Seine, the Esplanade du Général-de-Gaulle features a series of pedestrian paths around a mosaic-paved area in which a grass-covered roof by Fabio Rieti is set, hiding the stairs leading to one of the large car parks.

510-511

With a seating capacity of 80,000, the Stade de France in the suburb of Saint-Denis is the largest stadium in France. It was built by the SCAU and C.R. Architecture firms and inaugurated in 1998.

512 and 513

The view of the esplanade through the Arche de la Défense, designed by Danish architect Johann Otto von Spreckelsen and inaugurated in 1989, gives an idea of the technical feat achieved between 1956 and 1958, when the Centre National des Industries e des Tecniques. (CNIT) was built by Robert Edouard Camelot, Jean de Mailly and Bernard Louis Zehrfuss, with the engineer Jean Prouvé.

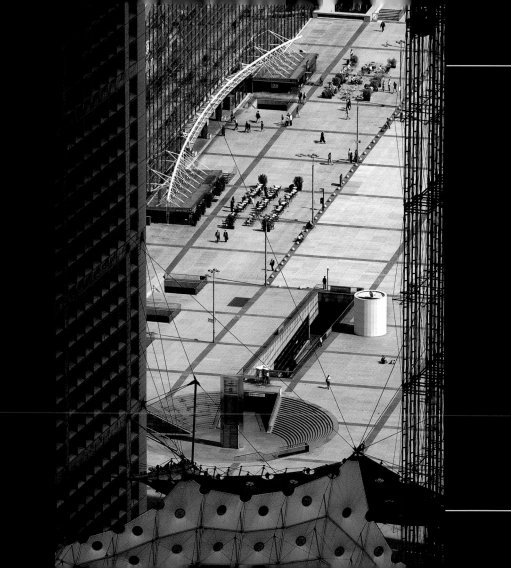

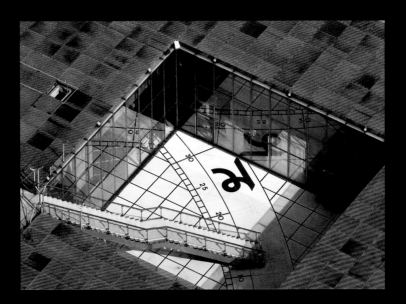

514

Just a few minutes from La Défense, the Nanterre-Préfecture district is home to the huge star-shaped Esplanade Charles-de-Gaulle.

515

Designed and created by Jean-Pierre Raynaud for the top of the Arche de la Défense, the *Carte du Ciel* ("Map of the Heavens") is formed by four marble patios.

Index

Index

Index

DOMINIQUE PAULVÉ IS A JOURNALIST AND WRITER. SHE CONTRIBUTES TO SPECIALIST ART PERIODICALS, SUCH AS CONNAISSANCE DES ARTS AND LA REVUE DE PIERRE BERGÉ & ASS. SHE IS INTRIGUED BY UNUSUAL PLACES AND HER PUBLICATIONS INCLUDE A WORK ON LA RUCHE, THE ARTISTS' SETTLEMENT BUILT IN 1900 USING MATERIALS SALVAGED FROM THE PARIS INTERNATIONAL EXPOSITION, AND LA CAMPAGNE À PARIS, IN WHICH SHE DISCOVERS THE HIDDEN PRIVATE GARDENS OF THE FRENCH CAPITAL. "FLYING HIGH" OFFERS AN OPPORTUNITY FOR HER TO CONTEMPLATE AN EVEN MORE SECRET PARIS: THE CITY AS VIEWED FROM A GREAT HEIGHT.

ACKNOWLEDGEMENTS

I WOULD LIKE TO THANK THE CHIEF OF POLICE AND HIS DEPARTMENT, AND THE GENERAL MANAGEMENT OF THE CIVIL AVIATION AUTHORITY FOR THE KIND AND EXTRAORDINARY AUTHORIZATION TO FLY OVER THE CITY. I WOULD ALSO LIKE TO EXPRESS MY GRATITUDE TO THE PRIME MINISTER'S SECRETARY, THE DOCUMENTATION FRAN_AISE, THE DEPARTMENT OF PHOTOGRAPHY, THE PARIS CITY PLANNING AUTHORITY AND, PARTICULARLY, MONSIEUR MILLIEX, HEAD ARCHITECT, AND MONSIEUR J.B. VAQUIN, FOR THEIR ENCOURAGEMENT. THANKS ALSO TO ROBERTO PETRONIO, FRANCK LECHENET, PHILIPPE PSA_LA, PAOLO MESTRE, THOMAS DESCHAMPS AND MY FRIEND AUGUSTO DA SILVA, WHO ACCOMPANIED ME THROUGHOUT ALL THESE FLIGHTS, FOR THEIR PRECIOUS COLLABORATION AND SUPPORT. FINALLY, HEARTFELT THANKS TO ALEXANDRE MILLERET FOR HIS PROFESSIONALISM AND HELPFULNESS, AND TO IXAIR AND HELIFRANCE.

PHILIPPE GUIGNARD

© 2007 WHITE STAR S.P.A.
Via Candido Sassone, 22-24
13100 Vercelli - Italia
WWW.WHITESTAR.IT

All photographs are by Philippe Guignard / air-images.net

TRANSLATION: SARAH PONTING

ISBN 978-88-544-0341-3

REPRINTS: 1 2 3 4 5 6   11 10 09 08 07

Printed in China
Color separation: Chiaroscuro, Turin

520
The Grande Arche de la Défense,
viewed from the outskirts about a
mile west of the capital, resembles
an immense white marble cube
facing the city.

FLYING HIGH